Wicked
BALTIMORE

CHARM CITY
SIN AND SCANDAL

LAUREN R.
SILBERMAN

THE
History
PRESS

Published by The History Press
Charleston, SC 29403
www.historypress.net

Cover images: The city of Baltimore City, Maryland, in 1880—view from the Washington
Monument looking south. A. Sachse & Co. Lithographers & Printers. *Courtesy of the Library
of Congress*; Portrait of Billie Holiday and Mister, Downbeat, New York, New York, circa
February 1947. *Courtesy of the William P. Gottlieb Collection, Library of Congress*; Baltimore,
Maryland Burlesque barker, by Marjory Collins, 1943. *Farm Security Administration/Office of
War Information Photograph Collection, Library of Congress.*

First published 2011
Second printing 2012
Third printing 2012

Manufactured in the United States

ISBN 978.1.60949.108.6

Library of Congress CIP data applied for.

Notice: The information in this book is true and complete to the best of our knowledge. It is
offered without guarantee on the part of the author or The History Press. The author and
The History Press disclaim all liability in connection with the use of this book.

Contents

CONTENTS

Baltimorbid

Long before "If it bleeds, it leads" became the journalistic credo of local TV news, a young, starving Baltimore poet learned pretty much the same lesson.

In the early 1830s, grave robbers were stealing teeth from corpses and selling them to dentists. The Baltimore papers reveled in the gory details. The more sensational the coverage, the more copies they sold.

Inspired by the gruesome news—and the public's appetite for it—our starving poet wondered if he could eke out a living applying his talent to more shocking subject matter. He penned a tale called "Berenice," about a guy obsessed with his cousin's teeth. After the cousin dies, the protagonist grabs some dental instruments, digs up her grave and yanks out her pearly whites—only to discover that she isn't quite dead.

The story was Edgar Allan Poe's first big hit as a writer; its success encouraged him to make tales of the "grotesque and arabesque" the financial mainstay of his literary career.

It is grisly historical anecdotes such as this—and other dark, lurid events chronicled in *Wicked Baltimore*—that give the Charm City a macabre kind of charm. Sure, I love the Inner Harbor, Fort McHenry and Camden Yards, but my telltale heart belongs to the morbid underbelly of Baltimore's history. Which makes my favorite attraction the old Western Burying Ground—now the Westminster Hall and Burying Ground—at Fayette and Greene Streets.

Established in 1786, Westminster is Baltimore's creepiest graveyard. Its ornate crypts and mausoleums reflect an early nineteenth-century fascination with Egyptology, reincarnation, premature burial and life after death. In 1852, a somber Gothic-style church was built on brick archways directly above the center portion of the graveyard, creating spooky catacombs in the basement. And Westminster Burying Ground is where the paths of two prominent figures in "Baltimorbid" intersect: Poe and a medical school janitor named Frank.

Edgar Allan Poe came from a Baltimore family and lived here from 1831 to 1835. His grandfather owned a burial plot near the back of the old Western Burying Ground, and Poe likely was in attendance when his tubercular brother, William Henry, was interred there in 1831. Poe joined him in 1849.

Poe's remains haven't remained still. In 1875, he was exhumed from his original unmarked grave and reburied not once, but twice, to make room for the large marble-and-granite memorial that now stands at the graveyard's northwest gate. If you think the supermarket tabloids go too far, check out what the *Baltimore Sun* wrote in 1875:

> *Nothing remained inside the coffin but the skeleton, all the flesh and grave clothes having long since returned to dust. Some hair yet attached to the skull, and the teeth, which appeared to be white and perfect, were shaken out of the jaws and lay at the bottom of the coffin.*

Poe's postmortem maneuverings led to wild conjecture that the gravediggers got the wrong body, which I debunked in a 2006 paper published by the Edgar Allan Poe Society of Baltimore. (See Ms. Silberman's chapter on Poe for more on his mysterious death and equally mysterious afterlife.)

I hate to admit it, but the possibility that grave robbers got to Poe's body shortly after it was buried cannot be ruled out. As demonstrated by the news story that served as a key source for "Berenice," grave robbing was a fact of life back then. It was especially big in Baltimore, where, according to one report, there was a "regular organization for the despoiling of graves. No grave, no matter how sacred or how greatly reverenced, was safe from these ravages."

Most body snatchers worked in secret. After all, plundering graves to supply cadavers for medical schools was a public relations no-no for the

8

sponsoring institutions, not to mention a serious crime. But one practitioner achieved a certain amount of professional fame in his day. His first name (we don't know his last name) was Frank.

Frank worked two blocks south of the Western Burying Ground, at the University of Maryland School of Medicine's Davidge Hall, during the early 1800s. He was the school's full-time janitor and part-time "resurrection" or "sack 'em up man,"—in other words, the resident body snatcher. (If he were working today, Frank might more accurately be termed a "covert interred remains retrieval technician.")

We know of Frank's existence through two letters written by a University of Maryland professor of surgery, Dr. Nathan Ryno Smith. In one letter, Dr. Smith bragged about Frank's skills. "A better one never lifted a spade," he wrote. Indeed, Frank must have been very good, for in an 1828 student recruitment catalogue, the University of Maryland described itself as "the Paris of America, where the subjects are in great abundance."

Apparently, bodies were in such great abundance that the university sold its surplus to other medical schools. Writing to a physician at Bowdoin College in Maine, Dr. Smith planned to send three cadavers pickled in whiskey: "I suppose they will require about half a barrel each, of whiskey; this at 35 cents a gallon, will be $16.80. The barrels a dollar each; the subjects, the putting up, etc., $10 each, making in all $50." After the medical school students unpacked the cadavers, they drank the whiskey. (Is that how rotgut whiskey got its name?)

This rather casual attitude about the illegal seizure and trafficking of human cadavers belies the fact that most professors and students were generally quite worried about how much the public knew of their doings. Baltimore was nicknamed "Mobtown," and mobs frequently gathered outside Davidge Hall and demonstrated against the dissections. In 1831, Dr. Smith wrote that Frank had been "greatly alarmed and fearful for his own personal safety and was not able to procure me a sufficient number of subjects for my demonstration."

Considering how prevalent body snatching was in Baltimore, I'm surprised Poe never used it as the basis for a story. Poe was a master at taking real events and shaping them into his own fiction. Take, for example, "The Premature Burial." Being buried alive was not something Poe made up. It actually happened. The papers were filled with stories—real or imagined—of people getting closed up in their coffins because they had the semblance of death. It was a common fear, and Poe merely exploited that fear for his story. The closest he came to writing about body snatching was in a minor tale called "Loss of Breath," also written in Baltimore, in which a conscious but catatonic man is dissected by a surgeon. Why Poe never wrote about grave robbing, I cannot say. Maybe body snatching was too pedestrian, an unpleasant fact of urban life—the nineteenth-century equivalent of getting one's car stolen. Or maybe, since the victims were already dead, it just didn't have that same element of fear of, say, premature burial. You'd think Poe could have written something really scary on the subject, but he didn't.

Poe's fame is secure. Frank, however, is a little-known footnote. I sought to change that in 1986, when I wrote and, along with actor Tony Tsendeas, first presented a short, one-man play about Frank (which, by the way, has been the featured attraction of the Westminster Hall and Burying Ground's Annual Halloween Tour every year since). In writing the script, I decided against making Frank a villain. Too often in horror movies the body snatcher is a bad guy, a monster, a sociopath, who, when he tires of digging up bodies, more expediently "creates" them by suffocation or other violent means. (See the chapter on "Burking.")

"I never resorted to murder," I had Frank say. "I always came by my bodies fairly."

My Frank is a kinder, gentler grave robber. He's interested in medicine. He enjoys the technical and physical challenge of shuttling 150 pounds of literal dead weight from graveyard to lecture hall without getting caught (his "graveside manner," he calls it). And while he takes pride in his contribution to medicine at large, he's quick to point out that others deserve most of the credit.

"The next time the doctor mends your broken arm, or makes your fever go away," Frank says, "don't forget the folks in the graveyard who gave so much of themselves."

It delights me to think that Baltimore's world-class medical reputation—Johns Hopkins, Ben Carson, Shock Trauma the Blue Baby Operations of Alfred Blalock and Vivien Thomas, to list but a few—has its origin in the clandestine, criminal and very dirty work of plucking corpses from freshly dug graves.

But then, as The History Press's Wicked series so vividly demonstrates, every city has some skeletons in its closet. In Baltimore, those skeletons are real.

Christopher Scharpf

Preface

I have always liked the sense of sin that emanates from Baltimore.
—*Russell Baker*[1]

Baltimore is truly a wicked place. From its nearly endless political rioting to the wink-eye of burlesque, the city encompasses the entire continuum of the word "wicked." Given its sordid history, visitors to Charm City might mistakenly believe that the city would hide its more salacious past, but Baltimore tends to embrace its darker side, such as when it enshrined Edgar Allan Poe's grave site and saved the once brothel-laden historic neighborhood of Fells Point. The citizenry here embrace their city's moniker of "Mobtown," enjoy marathons of John Waters's most scandalous films and hold annual festivals celebrating the privateers of yesteryear. However, no one has previously collected these scandalous stories into one succinct collection. *Wicked Baltimore* attempts to rectify this, bringing together some of the truly immoral stories from the city's early years.

Wicked Baltimore travels from the beginning of Baltimore in the eighteenth century to about the time Prohibition ended in 1933. While there are certainly more stories available than can fit in this little book, I tried to judiciously select among those of greater notoriety and intermingle them with some lesser-known tales of misconduct and unfortunate consequences. Throughout the book, readers will find famous names—from Betsy Bonaparte to Blaze Starr, from Frederick Douglass to Edgar Allan Poe and from Abraham Lincoln to

Al Capone—as well as people who may be unfamiliar to modern readers but have unforgettable stories, such as Emily Brown and Ellen Wharton.

Why do Baltimoreans embrace these stories today? They recognize that what makes Baltimore special isn't simply listing its positive merits. This is a city forged out of something more complex and more challenging than just its more praiseworthy accomplishments. Understanding and appreciating this heritage helps transform the city from a generic early American port to the quirky Charm City with its enviably distinct and complex cultural heritage. And besides, who doesn't enjoy a good, juicy story? Many of these stories provided strong fodder for the rumor mills of their day, and they have continued to hold up in interest and intrigue over time. For example, consider how many recent theories have been added to the litany of possibilities responsible for Poe's death—a man who died over 150 years ago.

These stories don't just reveal some distant past but also connect with the world today. Baltimore may have grown geographically and demographically from when it started in 1729, but at its heart, it's still strongly tied to the original sixty acres lining the water basin of the Inner Harbor—an area that features prominently in this book. So many of the riots included occurred along the waterfront, from the Pratt Street riots at the dawn of the Civil War to the start of the B&O Railroad riots in 1877, whose rage sparked a national outcry against unjust labor laws. The same area was home to several slave pens and auction sites before the Civil War, whose atrocities are highlighted in the second chapter. Nor is the waterfront far from "The Block," where a different sort of wicked spectacle occurred.

I researched *Wicked Baltimore* using a number of methods. Initially, I started with talking to historians, museum professionals and librarians to gather ideas and begin tracking down resources. Next came visiting several local museums and historic sites to see their materials on display and find out how they interpreted some of the stories I was interested in. The vertical files in the Maryland Room and African-American Room of the main branch of the Enoch Pratt Free Library (EPFL) were great starting points. I read some fantastic books and began culling through their endnotes for the original sources. The Maryland Historical Society (MDHS) has made all one hundred years of its journal available online, which proved invaluable. (Note that the most recent year is only available to society members.) Furthermore, Google Books and Archive.org have many materials in the public domain scanned and always accessible. Their issues of *Niles' Weekly Register* proved invaluable for Baltimore's early years.

The next step included tracking down the sources themselves. Anyone with an EPFL library card has access to its amazing databases, which includes free—and remote—access to the entire run of the *Sun*, as well as the *Afro-American* and other national papers, including the *Washington Post* and the *New York Times*. I was able to pull archival materials at MDHS and search the closed stacks of the EPFL's Maryland Room. The digital database of the Library of Congress (LOC) proved critical. In addition to searching for archival materials, I used LOC, MDHS and the Maryland Room—among others—for contemporary photographs. I'm thankful to everyone who shared resources and ideas with me. A full list of people I spoke with is included in the acknowledgements, and a list of materials is included in the bibliography. Sources throughout the book have been documented in endnotes.

I hope that people will enjoy *Wicked Baltimore*, learn more about this great city and maybe discover some stories they were unaware of. I have enjoyed researching and sharing these accounts and look forward to developing a dialogue about them. If readers have additional narratives to contribute, they can share them online at www.facebook.com/wickedbaltimore.

Acknowledgements

T his book wouldn't have been possible without the support of many fantastic people, in and beyond Baltimore. I have to start with Hannah Cassilly, my editor at The History Press, who provided great feedback and guidance. I am indebted to Christopher Scharpf for his fantastic foreword and endless well of information. Also, many thanks to the people who shared their ideas, pointed me to resources and gave suggestions: Wayne Schaumburg, Gil Sandler, Dean Krimmel, Johns Hopkins, Jayme Hill, Kate Marks, Heidi Glatfelter, Sherri Marsh, Melissa Rowell, Amy Lynwander, Mike Leister, Mike Connolly, Scott Clayton, Adam Jeffrey, Barbara Cromwell and Deb Weiner. Additionally, I wouldn't have made it very far without Jeff Korman and the rest of the librarians at the Enoch Pratt Free Library or Francis O'Neill and the librarians and volunteers at the Maryland Historical Society. Special thanks to Kristen Harbeson and Faye Rivkin for reading early drafts and providing feedback. Thank you to supporters of the project on Kickstarter.com, as well as the fans on the *Wicked Baltimore* Facebook page. And, of course, I couldn't do much of anything without my wonderful husband, Matt Moffett, or my loving family.

Banishing William Goddard

Having been this Morning assaulted when I was off my Guard, in my own House, by a Gang of Ruffians.
—*William Goddard, 1777*[2]

In 1777, William Goddard found himself banished from Baltimore. Again. As he traveled along the long route to Annapolis, he must have been fuming. Granted, his persecutors were the all-mighty Whigs—a club of the most powerful merchants in eighteenth-century Baltimore—but that would have provided only small solace. He had already been to the state legislature about them once, and the governor had even sided with him. How had he gotten himself into this mess? What was he going to do now?

Goddard originally came to Baltimore in 1773 to start its first newspaper: the *Maryland Journal and Baltimore Advertiser*. The small backwater city was growing, which promised the possibility of many new subscribers. True, John Adams would describe Baltimore as "the dirtiest city in the world" during the Second Continental Congress's winter sojourn there, but it was an untapped audience with great potential. Still, Goddard was someone who started more projects than he necessarily saw through. Just a year later, he would leave the newspaper to his sister, Mary Katherine Goddard, when he went to work with Benjamin Franklin on setting up the first national post office. But it wasn't a bad decision. Mary Katherine ran regular issues and helped the newspaper flourish. An accomplished printer herself, her name remained on the masthead even after he returned to the city.[3]

The trouble started in February 1777. The new nation was well into war with Britain, and Baltimore proved an incredibly patriotic town. Given how many of its early prominent families were Scots-Irish, it is probably not surprising that this enterprising town was not happy with the British status quo. The town's merchants had organized into a group called the Whigs, whose essential purpose was to "detect all traitors and discover all traitorous conspiracies against the State" and "to apprehend and bring to justice offenders" who would not have received their "deserved punishment from an unwillingness of individuals to interfere." In other words, the Whigs were a militia with a vendetta, and they were just waiting for someone to give them an excuse to exercise that "deserved punishment."[4]

Why did Goddard's newspaper come under scrutiny? Just a month earlier, Mary Katherine had published the first certified publication of the Declaration of Independence. Throughout the war, she would never miss a publication deadline. However, when her brother decided to print two satirical letters side by side on the front page of the paper, the Whigs took immediate notice.

Both letters were written by obvious pseudonyms. One, written by the so-called "Caveto," didn't pose any problems. The letter outlined all the evils the British brought to the country, extolling a Revolutionary fervor. He claimed that "the sun beholds not a more perfidious, corrupt and wicked people. My soul detests them as the gates of Hell." Caveto instructed readers to "shun any connexion with the people of Britain as with a common and infected prostitute."

The second letter, written by "Tom Tell-Truth," presented a problem. Instead of attacking "the insidious and wicked Court of Britain" as the first letter had, it actually praised the mother country and was strongly loyal to England. It reads as follows:

> For the MARYLAND JOURNAL, to the PRINTER.
> Through the channels of your paper, I take the liberty to congratulate my countrymen on the important intelligence, this day received by Congress. The terms of peace offered, by Howe, to America, manifest the magnanimity, generosity, and virtue of the British nation. The offer of peace, and, in return, to require only our friendship, and a preference

to our trade and commerce, bespeaks the ancient spirit of love and liberty, which were once the acknowledged and boasted characteristic of an Englishman. My soul overflows with gratitude to the patriotic virtuous King, the august incorruptible Parliament, and wise disinterested Ministry of Britain. I am lost in the contemplation of their private and public virtues. I disbelieve and forget, nay, will readily believe any assertion, that the monarch of Britain is a sullen and inexorable tyrant, the Parliament venal and corrupt, and the Ministry abandoned and bloody, as wicked and base calumnies. I am not able to express the feelings of my soul on the prospect of immediately seeing my native country blessed with peace and plenty. I am almost induced to complain of Congress, for concealing one moment these glad tidings: however, I will anticipate the pleasure, and claim thanks from all lovers of peace, for thus early communicating what may be relied upon as literally true.

Your's, &c.

TOM TELL-TRUTH

The second letter alarmed the Whigs. As the war raged on, here was an upstart printer who seemed to relish stirring up trouble. What would happen if people read this Tom Tell-Truth letter and agreed with it? Undoubtedly, there would be rioting and a total breakdown of support for the American cause. They weren't going to stand for such a flagrant violation of their beliefs and sought to root out the traitor from their midst. If the letter was meant to be ironic, the joke was lost on them.

The Whigs sent two of their members to visit Mary Katherine. As her name was on the masthead, any reader would assume that she made all the decisions. However, when they asked her to unmask the true identity of Tom Tell-Truth, she simply passed them along to her brother. He refused to cooperate. Unhappily, the Whigs left, but they weren't ready to give up. They sent Goddard a summons, requiring him to "answer such questions as may be asked him by the [Whig] club relative to a publication in the *Maryland Journal* of last week under the signatures of Tom Tell-Truth, which has given great offense to many of your Whig readers."[5]

Not surprisingly, he declined.

Undeterred, the Whigs sent a second summons—backed by a group of their followers. They took Goddard by force to their headquarters for an interrogation. When he refused to divulge the source of Tom Tell-Truth, they resolved that "Mr. William Goddard do leave this town by twelve o'clock to-morrow morning, and the County in three days—Should he refuse due obedience to this notice, he will be subject to the resentment of the Legion."[6]

Goddard had already tasted their resentment and immediately complied with their wishes. However, he didn't simply leave; he went straight to the state legislature to deal with this unruly "gang of ruffians." The state legislature and the governor concurred that the Whigs' actions were "a manifest violation of the constitution, directly contrary to the Declaration of Rights, and tend, in their Consequences (unless timely checked) to the Destruction of all regular Government."[7]

In response to the legislature's report, the Whigs responded with their own notice, declaring that their actions had been "grossly misinterpreted" and that they had only wanted to find the author because they were afraid that some people might have "overlooked the irony in Tom Tell-Truth, and mistaken it for a serious assertion of facts." According to them, Goddard had acted with "mulish obstinacy and brutal impoliteness" to their "gently entreaty." They wrote that they had simply recommended that he leave town because of his impertinent attitude.[8]

Goddard could not let the letter matter go and responded with an invective-filled pamphlet entitled *The Prowess of the Whig Club, and the Manoeuvres of Legion*. This greatly incensed the Whigs, who again summoned Goddard to meet with them. When he—again—refused, they once more took him against his will and banished him from Baltimore. Again.

Goddard didn't find such a receptive audience in Annapolis this time. While they found the matter in his favor, they also chided him that they'd prefer that he "give this house no more trouble, and that he be informed the courts of justice ever had been and still are open, where he may have his remedy, if injured." The legislature didn't have the time to continually handle such problems.[9]

Still, Goddard must have found solace in the statement from Governor Thomas Johnson, which he printed in his newspaper. Johnson declared that "all bodies of men associating together and meeting for the purpose and usurping any of the powers of government and presuming to exercise any power over the persons or property of any subject of this state, or to carry into execution any of the laws thereof on their own authority, unlawful assemblies." Even with this strong statement against personal vendettas and mob think, Goddard would soon find himself embroiled in scandal once more when he decided to publish another set of letters—although this time there was not even a hint of irony.

Two years later, Goddard found himself facing a new brew of trouble. Now it wasn't just the Whigs but a whole mob of angry readers congregating outside his front door. He feared that the "band of ruffians" would invade his house, seize him and do what horrible things he could hardly imagine. In a memoir, he wrote:

> *Under the shade of night, on the 8th [July] instant, at a late hour, when nature seemed hushed in silence and repose, this motley crew burst into the house of your memorialist, and entering his bedchamber, demanded his surrender and appearance before their main body, then assembled at the coffee-house, for the trial and punishment of your memorialist. Your memorialist had only time to snatch a sword from its scabbard and take a proper position for defense when he was pressed upon by this lawless band, who added insult to injury. Your memorialist, knowing himself to be answerable to no illegal tribunal, refused to obey the menacing summons he had received, and…entreated Capt. Cromwell, the leader of the party, not to put him to the fatal necessity of laying him dead at his feet, which should be his or any man's fate who ventured to seize on your memorialist.*[10]

Goddard never learned. Freedom of the press was not yet the quintessential right that we expect today, and Goddard saw his paper as a vehicle for whatever he wished to showcase. In June 1779, he readily agreed to print a series of questions from General Charles Lee, with whom he had personal and business relationships. As before, he printed the queries without revealing the author's true identity, although it would not have been difficult to ascertain. Goddard published the article entitled "Some Queries, Political and Military, Humbly Offered to the Consideration of the Public." The questions attacked General George Washington's reputation. It compared Washington's military failures to the more successful British maneuvers and campaigns and wondered whether Washington was really a fraud.

In the tenth and eleventh questions, the writer asked:

> *Whether, amongst the late warm, or rather loyal addressers, in this city, to his Excellency General Washington, there was a single mortal, one gentleman excepted, who could possibly be acquainted with his merits?*

Whether this gentleman excepted, does really think his Excellency a great man; or whether evidences could not be produced of his sentiments being quite the reverse?[11]

The questions continued building the case against Washington until reaching the final twenty-fifth one, which asked:

Whether it must not appear to every man who has read General Washington's letter to Congress, on the affair at Monmouth, and the proceedings of the Court-Martial, by which General Lee was tried, that if the contents of the former are facts, not only General Lee's defence [sic] must be a tissue of the most abominable audacious lies, but that the whole string of evidences, both on the part of the prosecution and prosecuted, must be guilty of rank perjury, as the testimonies of those gentlemen, near forty in number, delivered on oath, scarcely in one article coincide with the detail given in his Excellency's letter?

This last barb referred to General Lee's recent court-martial. He had overseen the Continental army's Monmouth campaign in 1778. The campaign failed, and Washington publicly reprimanded Lee on the battlefield. Offended, Lee argued back, attempting to defend himself. He followed up on the incident with a letter seeking a court of inquiry. Instead, Lee was court-martialed for "misbehavior before the enemy," among other accusations. Found guilty, Lee was suspended from command for a full year.

While Goddard may have suspected that the questions wouldn't go over well with the pro-Washington readers, he must have been taken aback by the contempt they caused. The mob dragged Goddard from his house and decided to parade him around the city with a rope hanging from his neck. He tried running to various people for support, but even the mayor of the city, James Calhoun, turned him down and ordered him to leave his premises. Later, Mayor Calhoun wrote to Governor Thomas Johnson about the incident. He described how "early in the morning, Goddard was seen parading in the streets with a Gun & his friend Coll. [Eleazer] Oswald with a drawn sword, venting his spleen in the most abusive language."[12]

Without support, Goddard relented. He agreed to print a supplement to his paper, recanting the published queries, and revealed the letter-writer to be General Charles Lee. While this somewhat appeased the mob, they still carted two of his sympathetic friends "with halters about their necks, and occasionally cudgeled for the diversion of the inhuman part of the spectators."[13]

Although he printed his apologies, Goddard quickly retracted his recantation. The incident left him upset, and he wrote:

> *I had like to have been mobbed to death by a parcel of Poltroon* [sic] *officers, Blackguard Continental Soldiers, & Negroes, Headed by Coll. Smith, and the damn'd rascally Magistrates of Baltimore would not give me any redress I will seek it to the farthest end of the world, yes I will take up the Tomahawk and Scalping knife and will be worse than any Hessian or Waldecker.*[14]

Goddard continued to publish, even as his readers continued to dog him. Even his relationship with his sister grew strained, and they began competing against each other. He attacked her character and reputation. She dropped her name from the newspaper and sold her share of it. In 1792, Goddard left the paper—and Baltimore—for Rhode Island. His sister didn't follow, remaining in Baltimore until her death in 1816.

Still, in many ways, Goddard was an early pioneer who refused easy categorization. Even today, historians debate about his political stances and whether he deserved more recognition for his involvement in establishing the postal system. Either way, he left a lasting impact on Baltimore, which was soon home to several newspapers. Even so, the growing city would not quickly shed its frontier mentality or vicious mob, which would only escalate in the new century.

Napoleon's Sister-in-Law

The International Marriage Scandal of Betsy Patterson Bonaparte

Your marriage is null both in a religious and legal point of view. I will never acknowledge it.
—*Emperor Napoleon to Betsy Patterson Bonaparte, undated*[15]

Being the "Belle of Baltimore" was apparently not good enough for Napoleon Bonaparte. Perhaps if he had actually encountered Elizabeth "Betsy" Patterson, he may have swooned in the same manner as had his younger brother, Jerome. However, the emperor kept the young woman as far from him as possible and resisted her charms, her intelligence and her ambitions. Napoleon had an empire to run, and after Betsy married Jerome, he knew she would only be trouble.

Everything started in 1803, when Jerome Bonaparte found himself in America. Having fared poorly in the French navy in the West Indies and concerned that the British would nab him on his journey home to France, he instead took a leisurely journey across the young country. He continually said that he was waiting for orders from his brother before acting, knowing that it would take a minimum of two months to send notice across the ocean and receive anything in response. He repeatedly ignored orders from his military superiors, continuing to hold fast to the idea that his brother would instruct him. Jerome was young, impetuous and ready to enjoy whatever bounties America offered. He was notoriously generous and a big spender, always exceeding the allowances his family made available to him.

He was also friends with Commodore Joshua Barney, a Revolutionary War hero who had served in the French navy and worked with Bonaparte. Barney invited Bonaparte to stay with him at his home in Baltimore. At some point during his stay, he saw—and immediately fell for—Betsy Patterson. Born in 1785, Betsy was the daughter of William and Dorcas Spears Patterson. A successful businessman, William was the second richest man in Maryland, after Charles Carroll of Carrollton, and as such, Betsy grew up without want. Perhaps that is why she was able to wear the "buff-colored silk dress and a hat with long ostrich plumes" on the day that Bonaparte first laid eyes upon her, instantly catching his attention.[16]

According to Eugene Didier, who published a book of Betsy's letters, the younger Bonaparte laid eyes on Betsy during the fall horse races, where "the impulsive young Frenchman was fired at once. He declared enthusiastically, that he had never beheld so lovely a being before." However, Didier says that they weren't introduced until a few days later, during a ball at Judge Samuel Chase's home. Chase was also Commodore Barney's father-in-law. According to legend, Patterson's necklace caught on Bonaparte's button while they danced—meaning that their destinies would be eternally entangled.[17]

McBride's magazine shared a more romanticized version, claiming that while Jerome was in Martinique, he complained to a woman that he would never find someone to marry. Being from Baltimore, the anonymous woman responded that she knew "the most beautiful woman in the world," referring to Betsy. He was immediately intrigued and set off for America.[18]

Betsy, on the other hand, shared an entirely different version of their initial meeting, which she said was at a dinner party held by Albert Gallatin, the former secretary of the treasury. In this account, Betsy and her friend Henrietta Pascault saw two men approach the house. Henrietta pointed at the taller gentleman, saying that she would marry him. Betsy agreed and said she would take the other man. Accordingly, both did exactly as they predicted, with Henrietta marrying Jean-Jacques Reubell and Betsy tying the knot with Jerome Bonaparte.[19]

While Betsy's father was originally against the marriage, he eventually consented, and the two were married on December 24, 1803. Betsy was eighteen, and Jerome had just turned nineteen. Having already introduced her to the latest European fashions, the beautiful Betsy undoubtedly turned heads when she appeared in her wedding dress. One attendee was said to remark that "he could have put all that she had on in his vest pocket."[20]

When Napoleon learned of the wedding, he was furious. The recently crowned emperor turned to Pope Pius VII to annul it. However, Bishop John Carroll had performed the nuptials, and the pope considered the marriage legitimate. Using a plural first person point of view, he wrote a lengthy response to Napoleon, explaining his inability to undo the marriage—a response that Betsy kept a copy of in translation:

> *It is not in our power to give the judgment of nullity…If we were to usurp an authority, which does not belong to us, we should be guilty of the most abominable abuse of our sacred ministry before the tribunals of G-d and the whole church. Your majesty should be displeased if we were to pronounce a judgment contrary to the dictates of our conscience and to the invariable principles of the Church. Thus, we hope ardently that your Majesty will…accept this declaration as a sincere evidence of our paternal affection.*[21]

Under French law of the time, the younger Bonaparte was considered a minor and needed parental permission to get married. Although the pope did not see that as an impediment to the legitimacy of the union, Napoleon did. He began looking for new ways to bring his brother back to France and to undo the match.

Meanwhile, Jerome assured Betsy that his brother would come around, and in an optimistic spirit, they decided to sail to Europe, even though she was already pregnant with their son. When the ship docked in Lisbon, Portugal, Jerome set off across the mainland to convince his brother, leaving his pregnant wife docked at sea. Unbeknownst to either of them, it would be the last time they would see each other for decades.

Napoleon would not be swayed and managed to change his brother's mind by offering him his own kingship of the newly created country of Westphalia. Betsy was left virtually alone, trying unsuccessfully to find a way onto land, but Napoleon had ordered all ports to block her ship from docking and disembarking. Seeing no other alternative, she turned to the long-standing French enemy: England. Newspapers regularly documented her journey across Europe and America. She gave birth to her son, Jerome Napoleon Bonaparte, on July 7, 1805, near London.

Meanwhile, her family argued for her to return to Baltimore, but Betsy found that impossible. She had almost touched the life of European royalty and, as a result, saw her hometown existence as provincial. Her son was a potential heir to the empire—how could she return? For although Napoleon had broken her marriage, and although her husband was now married to a foreign princess, she kept her attention on the bigger picture of her son becoming next in line to the throne and eventually marrying someone of stature.

Napoleon wrote to Betsy, ordering her to return to America. He offered her an annual pension of 60,000 francs if she returned and dropped her married name. He wrote:

> *I have received your letter of this morning. There is no fault that you have committed which may not be effaced in my eyes by a sincere repentance. Your marriage is null both in a religious (a lie) and legal point of view. I will never acknowledge it.*[22]

The "a lie" is Betsy's annotation. She copied the letter into her letter book, which she maintained over several years.

The issue would never be fully resolved. Betsy spent years in both America and Europe, trying to win over support for her claim. Although she garnered many admirers, she never remarried and even won a divorce in Maryland so that she could maintain the properties and investments she had acquired. State law would have given those materials to her husband, even if his family didn't acknowledge the marriage.

In 1822, Betsy encountered her former husband and his wife, Princess Catherine of Württemberg, in the Pitti Palace in Florence, Italy. Not a word was spoken between them, and Jerome hurried off, reportedly whispering, "That is my American wife." They left Italy the next morning. According to historian Helen Jean Burn, before Jerome could leave the museum, Betsy flung open her cloak, showcasing the remarkable figure that she had maintained over the years. In stark contrast, his current wife was apparently quite obese and no longer the arresting beauty that Betsy continued to be.

Although neither Betsy nor her descendants ever won their claim, they did prosper. When Betsy died in 1879, she had accumulated over $10 million in investments. Her son had married and started a family of his own. While the American Bonaparte line eventually disappeared, the European line continues unabated. Recently, renewed interest in Betsy's life has sparked

Betsy Bonaparte's tomb at Greenmount Cemetery. *Author photograph.*

several biographies, and many still make the trip to mark the grave of the princess-to-be in Greenmount Cemetery in downtown Baltimore.

While she may not have found a throne, she has carved out a permanent place in history by becoming the woman who captivated a royal, incensed an emperor and fascinated the world.

America's Oldest Operating Penitentiary

As drivers sail down I-83, which bisects the heart of the city, they will undoubtedly pass a large concrete slab of a building just before the expressway ends. This imposing structure is the long-serving Maryland Penitentiary. Opened in 1811, it is the oldest operating penitentiary in the country—and perhaps in the world. A penitentiary is not to be confused with a prison, which was designed as a place of "simple confinement." The concept of a penitentiary as providing a place of reflection and reform started during the Age of Enlightenment. Baltimore's was the second of its kind constructed in the country, after Eastern State Penitentiary in Philadelphia opened in the late eighteenth century.[23] While Baltimore's penitentiary continues to function, Eastern State is now a museum.

Construction started in 1804, but the building didn't open until 1811. Unfortunately, this was too late for night watchman George Workner, who was killed during an escape attempt from Baltimore's old jail in 1808. A prisoner known only as Moses had managed to fashion a key for the cell doors, and on the evening of March 14, nine prisoners broke free. During the ensuing mêlée, they wounded several guards and knifed Workner in his side. However, their freedom didn't last long; all were eventually recaptured. Four of the recaptured men—Daniel Doherty, William Morris, Caleb Doherty and William Robinson—were convicted of Workner's murder and hanged in the jail yard on April 22, 1808.[24]

Not that there were not escape attempts and riots after the penitentiary was opened. The worst riot occurred over one hundred years later, in

August 1920—less than a month after the death of longtime warden John F. Leonard. On Monday, August 16, seven hundred prisoners protested their "monotonous food" by striking in the prison shops. Interim warden Patrick J. Brady attempted to quell any violence by refusing to feed them anything until they returned to work. Many relented, and the holdouts were isolated in a different dormitory. On Friday, August 20, in the early morning hours, fifty-nine of the holdouts started rioting. They "went on a rampage, ripping heavy metal doors off hinges, breaking furniture, prying bricks from the walls and hurling them through the windows." The battle lasted over five hours before peace was restored.[25]

The greatest escape artist of the penitentiary was Jack Hart, leader of a gang that killed William D. Norris, a contractor, in 1922. A group of five men killed Norris at the corner of Madison Street and Park Avenue in Mount Vernon. They made off with Norris's $7,263 payroll. The other men included Walter Socolow, who was the one to shoot Norris; John Smith; Charles Carey; and Frank Allers.[26]

During Hart's internment, he continually plotted various escape methods. Like Houdini, he was often successful with his off-the-wall schemes. In his first year behind bars, authorities found him inside a hole he had dug into the prison wall. They found him with crackers, cigarettes, matches and rope. In 1924, he succeeded in escaping after using an iron piece to bend window bars. William F. Gilbson, another inmate, escaped with him. Hart's freedom lasted most of the year. He was recaptured in Chicago after a $35,000 silk warehouse robbery. He didn't give up. Less than six months later, he created a key with William Fergus, also interned, to unlock the tier door. Fergus had made a knife from a file. After being caught, Hart tried cutting his way out through the slate floor. He had managed to cut 1.8 inches deep and 7.0 inches wide. In 1928, he cut a hole in a water tank. That same year, authorities found a saw in his cell.[27]

In 1929, Hart managed to get through his solitary confinement cell's three locks. After helping free George Bailey, the duo used a can opener to cut into the ventilating system. From there, they absconded to the roof and descended down the Eager Street side of the penitentiary using a rope made of bedsheets and ticking. Only Hart made it. The rope broke, leaving Bailey behind. Hart wouldn't be recaptured for four years—again in Chicago. San Francisco cops had caught up with him in 1930, when they arrested him for theft, but Hart posted bail and fled. The Chicago authorities arrested him for wounding three men in 1933. He had been posing as James Kelly and working as a hustler for a racing stable. He remained in Joliet Prison until being paroled in 1934. At that point, he was returned to Baltimore to serve out the remainder of his term. Not surprisingly, he made several more attempts at escape but was never again successful.[28]

Hart made several attempts at pleading for parole, which he was finally granted in 1955. He was sixty-five when released. He was the only gang member from the initial murder left in the penitentiary. Socolow, the shooter, was paroled after serving his full sentence. Smith died in 1946 in the state reformatory in Hagerstown, Maryland. Carey was hanged after killing a prison guard in a botched escape attempt. Another inmate murdered Allen on the day before he was set to be released.[29]

According to another tale, the penitentiary's very existence played a role in converting a young man into a criminal. William "Jerry" Blaney was only about eleven years old when he watched two men—Joshua Nicholson and Thomas Holloway—hang in the yard at the city jail, next to the penitentiary. How that event transformed the boy is unknown, but it certainly transfixed him.[30]

At around the age of twenty-five, Blaney would go on to murder his grandmother and his aunt—Sarah and Caroline Blaney, respectively— with an axe handle. He had been a favorite of his grandmother's and regularly visited her and his aunt at their ramshackle home on Greenmount Avenue. Fourteen-year-old Milton Abbott saw a drunken Blaney and another man talk before Blaney entered the home on the night of the murder. Abbott heard one of the women inside scream. He identified Blaney the next day in the station house. The police found blood smeared on his pants and on a monetary note he carried. He claimed that the stains had come from a nosebleed.[31]

According to his prosecutors, Blaney killed the women because his aunt had loaned his grandmother money to purchase a stall in a market. She had recently sold a house and had come into a large sum of money. The upstairs of the house was ransacked. He apparently didn't find the $900 on his aunt's body. He was found guilty of the crime and sentenced to hang. He attempted escape in April but was found the next day. On June 12, 1891, Blaney was hanged in the same yard as the two men he saw die more than a decade earlier.[32]

Today, the facility is known as the Metropolitan Transition Center (MTC) and operates under the Department of Public Safety and Correctional Services. MTC staff work with the Baltimore Pre-Release Unit, Baltimore City Correctional Center and two community adult rehabilitation centers. MTC has an average daily population of 786 inmates.[33]

The Birth of Mobtown

The direful Mob was heard to shout—We'll drink their blood! We'll root them out!
—Pamphlet, September 1, 1812

B altimore has at its disposal a generous host of nicknames, from the enlightened "Monument City," "Charm City" and the "City of Firsts" to the more salacious "Syphilis City" and "BodyMore" (referring to the city's historically high murder rate). However, no name has resonated with the city more than its early nineteenth-century moniker of "Mobtown." The label stems from a riot begun in the dawning hours of the War of 1812. Just as the citizenry had been strongly patriotic during the Revolutionary War, Baltimore retained this fervor during the rematch between America and England. Even well before the war began, Baltimoreans were protesting new British taxes. In September 1808, the brig *Sophia* left Holland for the city carrying 720 gallons of Geneva gin. The British overtook the ship, forcing the crew to pay a cargo tax before allowing it to continue on its voyage. When Baltimore's citizenry heard what had happened, they reacted the way they knew best: by rioting.[34]

When the *Sophia* reached its port, the mob decided to burn its contents. The owner of the ship relented to the masses, allowing the contents to be "condemned to the flames."[35] The rioters organized a large parade with twelve hundred horsemen, four hundred sailors and five hundred citizens. They even created a wheeled barge festooned with banners reading,

A view of the bombardment of Fort McHenry, near Baltimore, by the British fleet, by J. Bower, circa 1816, *Library of Congress.*

"Bunker Hill Forever!" "Liberty of the Seas, Huzzah!" and "No Tribute!" As the parade surged east to Hampstead Hill, it merged with another fifteen thousand people and formed a giant ring. Within the circle, a gallows was constructed for the gin. They attached a flag, inscribed "British Orders of the Council." As a band played "Yankee Doodle," the gin was burned.[36]

Not everyone shared such a loyal view on the new war, which began officially on June 18, 1812. A group of Federalists loudly opposed the war. A newspaper called the *Federal Republican*, run by Alexander Contee Hanson, openly condemned it in an editorial written on June 20. In return, a mob ripped apart his Gay and Second Street shop on June 22. During the looting and destruction, one person fell through a window to his death. According to John Fleming in a deposition, the "Mayor, the Judge of the Criminal Court, and several other Magistrates and Police Officers" witnessed the destruction without doing anything. Fearing for his life, Hanson fled to Georgetown, where he resumed publication. After a few weeks, he returned to Baltimore, setting up in a friend's house at 45 South Charles Street. According to a contemporary, anonymous letter published on August 13 in the *Hampden Federalist*, a Massachusetts newspaper, Hanson was prepared for trouble. He wrote:

> [He] *had furnished* [the house] *with arms and ammunition, in the expectation that it would be attacked, and with the determination to defend it. Mr. H*[anson] *was accompanied to town by several friends from Montgomery County; among others were Gen. Lignan, a venerable old gentleman, about sixty-five years of age; Gen. Lee, a revolutionary officer, and the bosom friend of Washington; Dr. Warfield; Mr. Murray, a brother in law of Mr. H. and several others. These gentlemen remained to protect him, should it be necessary.*

"Gen. Lignan" was General James McCubbin Lignan, a distinguished veteran of the Revolutionary War who had fought at the Battles of Long Island and Fort Washington and survived the British prison ship *Jersey*. "Gen. Lee" was none other than General Richard Henry "Light-Horse Harry" Lee, a veteran and father of the future Confederate general Robert E. Lee. He had been the one honored to eulogize President Washington as "first in peace, first in war, and first in the hearts of his countrymen." "Mr. Murray" was Daniel Murray.

The group's suspicions proved correct. After dusk fell on July 27, a mob of about thirty men congregated outside the house. Words were exchanged, and the group outside grew in size and agitation. Soon, they started throwing stones at the house and attempted to break down the door. According to the letter writer, "Windows and sashes and shutters were demolished in an instant, while bricks and paving stones were flying about our heads with the most tremendous crash."[37] The Federalists returned volley, firing into the air and killing one person outside, Dr. Thaddeus Gale. According to reports, the mob even brought a cannon to the scene, although it was never fired.

In the middle of the night, the militia, led by Major William B. Barney (son of notable Baltimore privateer Joshua Barney), arrived in an attempt to restore order. A tentative peace lasted for a few short hours, and a who's who of Baltimore authorities—including Mayor Edward Johnson, General John Stricker and more—attempted to convince the Federalists to leave the house for the purported safety of the local jail. Although the group initially protested, they were eventually convinced to leave.

The group was held in the city jail against their will and safety. By nightfall, the general, mayor and others left them alone without protection. According to one of the group's members, John Thomson:

About dark the back door of the gaol [jail] was beset by the Mob, who entered it without breaking it by force. By whom it was opened I do not know, but by hearsay. They began to break down the wood and iron gratings in the passage leading to our room, which took them at least three quarters of an hour. They had the light of torches.[38]

The group inside the jail resolved to rush the door as soon as it was opened, extinguishing the lights on the way. They didn't have long to wait. "The grating of our room was opened instantly without any exertion," Thomson continued, "which makes me believe it was opened by some one having the key." While he and Daniel Murray wanted to shoot at the intruders with a pistol he had, General Lignan argued against it, afraid that shooting would incite the mob even further.[39]

As the door opened, the group ran for their lives. Several initially escaped but were pointed out by a butcher named Mumma. Thomson was "struck on the back of my head with a heavy club by some man I had passed, which threw me forward from the head of the steps, and I fell headlong down about twelve feet." The "gang of ruffians" outside tarred and feathered him as they continued to beat him and attempted to gouge his eyes and break his legs with iron bars. He attempted to play dead, but someone set fire to the tar and feathers, forcing him to roll over. As they continued their torture, he was forced into revealing his companions' names before finally being carted to a hospital.[40]

According to another account, the mob was "sticking pen-knives into [the prisoners'] faces and hands, and opening their eyes and dropping hot candle-grease into them."[41] Unknown "noblemen" assisted the anonymous letter writer's escape after he failed at playing dead. Murray also tried to play dead, but someone pushed a stick down his throat. Several others were pushed down the jail's steps, where they remained for nearly three hours. Some managed to escape unhurt, but they were the lucky few.

General Lee was almost blinded in his right eye, and his face was scarred. A friend said that "his head was cut to pieces." General Lignan argued for his life, crying out "that he had fought for their liberties throughout the Revolutionary War." Instead of sympathy, a rioter responded, "He is one of those damn'd rascals who came from a distance to murder our citizens, no matter what he was formerly, he is a damn'd tory now, he ought to be put to death!" Unfortunately, General Lignan died from the resulting beating.

While Hanson survived the attack, his injuries were severe. He wrote in a letter on August 3:

> *I have six wounds on the head, either of which, sufficiently severe to induce an inflammation of the brain, without great care. Both collar bones are hurt. The extremity of the spinal bone injured, and excessively painful.—The breast bruised, and now painful. The fore finger of the right hand broken, and the whole hand injured having been twice stabbed, once through, with a pen knife; and the nose broken.—These are the injuries I have received, but they do not give me half the pain that the despondency of my political friends (in Baltimore) inflicts.*[42]

Sympathy to his and the others' plight eventually served in Hanson's favor, as he went on to be elected to Congress in Montgomery County as the Federal party came to power across the state. Still, he remained plagued by his injuries for the remainder of his life, dying in 1819 at the age of thirty-three.

The riot only proved to be one in a long secession of political violence in the city. As will be discussed more in a later chapter, the citizens of Baltimore tended to hold deep beliefs that they often defended with their lives. While reformers regularly responded to these crises with calls for moderation, it would be decades before they were heard. As the city grew at a quickened pace, people encountered others with different sets of core values. Rather than learn from one another and discover a middle ground through peaceable means, they instead continued to use force as the main measure for responding to changes—in both Baltimore and the country at large. In essence, the city suffered from growing pains. As a result, lives were lost, but eventually new methods would come about to replace the old. Just not in Hanson's lifetime.

Nest of Pirates

[This] *nest of pirates* [that is, Fells Point, Baltimore] *would be shaken with*
weapons that shook the city of Copenhagen.
—Evening Star, *London, reprinted in* Niles' Weekly Register, *Baltimore,*
April 3, 1813

As the War of 1812 picked up steam, the British gunned for Fells Point, Baltimore's major nautical center. They had already deemed the area to be a lowly "nest of pirates" during the Revolutionary War, and now Baltimore was an even fiercer competitor. America's navy was birthed in Fells Point's clipper ships—small but fast topsail schooners that easily outmaneuvered the big, bumbling ships of war out of England. The country's first two naval ships—the *Wasp* and the *Hornet*—came from this growing port. Still, the official navy was tiny compared to the vast and experienced English fleet. To make up the difference, the government began, in 1776, to issue "letters of marque" to private ship captains, also known as privateers. Technically, these letters only allowed the captains to ready their ships for self-defense, but many used them as an excuse to attack and loot British ships. Historian John Thomas Scharf considered the privateers to be "nurse of the infant Navy."

During the War of 1812, the Baltimore clipper *Nonsuch* was the first to be commissioned as a letter of marque and was soon followed by over forty more privateers. The *Dolphin* sent the first prize back to Baltimore. It took twelve vessels, bringing in over $54,000. All together, the letters of marque captured—or sank—a reported seventeen hundred British ships. Only ten were captured or run aground by the British, and only one was lost at sea.

The most daring of the privateers was the famed Thomas Boyle. Though born in Massachusetts, Boyle came to Baltimore in the late 1700s and married a local woman. He soon rose to fame for captaining the *Comet*, which captured thirty-five vessels on three cruises and grossed over $400,000 in prizes. In 1814, he commanded the best ship in the fleet, the famous *Chasseur*, which featured two Long Toms, sixteen guns and 120 men. The British called it the "Phantom Ship." Boyle enjoyed taunting the British by sailing around their slower ships. Every time they attempted to fire on him, he'd simply move out of range quicker than they could maneuver. When he moved in for the kill, he would fire a single, close-range broadside. As chaos erupted aboard the enemy ship, his crew would board the ship and take it over before anyone knew what had happened.

Two British admirals, John Barlaise Warren and Alexander Cochrane, had issued a "paper blockade" of the entire American coastline, which instructed British ships to block all of the country's waterways. Boyle recognized the ridiculousness of the plan, given the country's vast geographic size. In rebuke, he took it upon himself to head straight for England. After arriving, he immediately captured the local brig, the *Marquis of Cornwallis*, so as to send a notice to the entire country—including the king and the offending admirals. The notice was nailed to the doors of the shipping underwriters, Lloyd's Coffee House (now Lloyd's of London). The proclamation claimed that his one ship was to embargo the entire country:

> *I do, therefore, by virtue of the power and authority in me vested (possessing sufficient force) declare all the ports, harbors, bays, creeks, rivers, inlets, outlets, island and sea coasts of the United Kingdom of Great Britain and Ireland in a state of strict and rigorous blockade, and I do further declare that I consider the forces under my command adequate to maintain strictly, rigorously and effectually, the said blockade…And, I hereby caution and forbid the ships and vessels and every nation, in amity and peace with the United States, from entering or attempting to come out any of the said ports, harbors, bays, creeks, rivers, inlets, outlets, islands, or sea coasts, on or under any pretense whatever; and that no person may plead ignorance of this my proclamation, I have ordered the same to be made public in England.*[43]

Knowing his audacious feats and wily methods, Lloyd's immediately raised insurance rates, essentially grounding many ships. The Admiralty was forced to call back its own war ships to protect its merchant fleet. Furthermore, Boyle followed true to his threat by capturing or sinking seventeen British ships. He only quit after he ran out of crew to command the prize vessels. Given his stunning success, the ship went on to be known as the "Pride of Baltimore." A replica of the ship, the *Pride of Baltimore II*, sails out of Baltimore's Inner Harbor today.

Besides Boyle, Baltimore boasted another famous privateer: Commodore Joshua Barney. He was born in the city in 1759 and was soon an apprentice on a brig headed to England. Recognized for his nautical prowess, he became second mate at only fourteen. At sixteen, Barney found himself in control after the captain died and the first mate abandoned the ship. Not to mention, the ship was leaking. Still, he managed to successfully lead the sinking ship to Gibraltar.[44]

During the Revolutionary War, he served on both the *Hornet* and the *Wasp* and went on to become a lieutenant in the fledgling navy. Even though he was personally captured twice—and released—by the British, he nonetheless managed to capture several of their ships. After the war, he joined the French navy for a few years, which is how he came into contact with Jerome Bonaparte (which was discussed in an earlier chapter).

Although he had officially retired from the service by 1812, Barney took up the mantle when called as America engaged the British again. He took control of the *Rossie* in July 1812. Over the following ninety days, he captured, sank or otherwise destroyed eighteen British ships—worth approximately $1.5 million—and took about 217 men prisoner.[45] In 1813, he was offered command of the Chesapeake flotilla, which he readily accepted. When they set sail in 1814, he commanded twenty-six gunboats and barges, as well as about 900 men. He engaged in fierce battles with the British, including action with the *Dragon*, a seventy-four-gun ship. His biographer, Mary Barney, described what happened, writing:

> *He was closely pursued by the whole force of the enemy, and before he reached the Patuxent [River], one of the schooners, mounting eighteen guns, and several of the barges, had approached within gunshot of his flotilla—the* Dragon *being still at a distance, he made the signal for action, and a fire was opened from all the flotilla, which in a few minutes*

compelled the enemy to seek protection under the battery of the seventy four; having thus driven them from his heels, he entered the river in safety, and the Dragon and her attendants took post at its mouth.[46]

The battle went back and forth for several days until the "grand attack" on June 10:

> *Twenty-one barges, one rocket boat, and two schooners* [of the British fleet], *each mounting two thirty-two pounders, with eight hundred men, entered the creek with colors flying, and music sounding its animating strains, and moved on with the proud confidence of superiority. Barney's force consisted of thirteen barges, and five hundred men—his sloop and two gun vessels being left at anchor above him, as unmanageable in the shoal water—but he did not hesitate a moment to accept the challenge offered, and gave the signal to meet the enemy, as soon as they had entered the creek.*[47]

Barney and his son, William B. Barney, "were seen rowing about everywhere…giving the necessary orders to the flotilla."[48] The battle went back and forth, but the Americans held their own, even with the smaller force.

In a later battle, Barney was struck in the leg, and no one was able to extract the ball from his bone. Eventually, this wound would exacerbate the illness that would claim his life in 1818.

With the daring privateers, growing navy, strong troops at North Point and Hampstead Hill and well-defended Fort McHenry, Baltimore was able to hold off the British's proposed attack on Fells Point and other neighborhoods. While the British hampered privateering, they didn't succeed in stopping these wily, successful men. The captains used other cities as temporary ports and shipped their goods back to Baltimore overland instead. After the war, many of the ships were converted into trade vessels, which carried materials as far away as China. They were soon known as "opium clippers" because of how many carried the drug. Given their speed and size, several became active in the illegal international slave trade, as they could outmaneuver the naval ships.

Fort McHenry remained a well-known base of defense during the War of 1812. Francis Scott Key wrote the poem "Defenders of Fort McHenry," later known as "The Star-Spangled Banner," while on a boat outside Fort

"Star Spangled Banner," transcribed for the piano by Charles Voss, circa 1861. *Copyright by G. Andre & Co.; Lithograph by P.S. Duval & Son after drawing and lithograph by J. Queen. Library of Congress.*

McHenry during Britain's unsuccessful attempt to destroy the star-shaped fort. Lesser known is the origin of the anthem's melody, which originates in a song called "To Anacreon in Heaven," originally composed by John Stafford Smith in the 1700s for the Anacreontic Club, which gathered to sing and drink at the Crown and Anchor Tavern in England (and perhaps pinch a few serving wenches while at it!). The society was formed in homage to Anacreon, a Greek lyric poet, and was devoted to "wit, harmony, and the god of wine." Its president, Ralph Tomlinson, wrote the lyrics, which imagine the club's mythological creation. The song was popular in its day and was likely known by Key. The first verse goes as follows:

> *To Anacreon in Heav'n, where he sat in full glee,*
> *A few Sons of Harmony sent a petition;*
> *That he their Inspirer and Patron wou'd be;*
> *When this answer arrived from the Jolly Old Grecian;*
> *"Voice, Fiddle, and Flute,*

No longer be mute,
I'll lend you my name and inspire you to boot,
And besides I'll instruct you like me, to intwine,
The Myrtle of Venus with Bacchus's Vine."

Just a few weeks after Key wrote "Defenders of Fort McHenry," an actor named Harding at Baltimore's Holliday Street Theater sang it to the tune of "To Anacreon in Heaven." After he finished, the company reenacted the bombing of Fort McHenry.[49]

After the war, Fort McHenry continued to serve an important military function and was even a prison during the Civil War. Each year, the city remembers the attack during Defender's Day at the fort. Across the water, the neighborhood of Fells Point grew and soon became an important port for trade and immigration. Today, much of the historic character of the area remains intact, and it is a popular tourist destination.

A Terrible Trade

The Slave Pens of Baltimore

*The feeling was very bitter toward all colored people in Baltimore, about this time, and
they—free and slave—suffered all manner of insult and wrong.*
—Frederick Douglass

*NEGROES WANTED—Having returned from New Orleans, I will now pay the
highest cash prices for all likely negroes that are slaves for life and good titles. All
communications will be promptly attended to.*
—Hope H. Slatter, Pratt Street

As the nineteenth century pushed along, Baltimore continued its quick-paced rise from being a pre–Revolutionary War backwater to one of the largest cities in the country. As the city became more urbanized, it also became more desirable for people to move there. Visitors remarked on its development, including Irish actor Tyrone Power, who, when visiting in the early 1830s, wrote, "As a residence I like Baltimore much; its market is equal to any other in the States, and cheaper than either Philadelphia or New York."[50] Some of these visitors stayed permanently, making the emerging city their home. Among the groups coming to Baltimore was one that would find it to be a place of both opportunity and torment: African American men and women.

Baltimore had the largest population of free blacks in the country. Between 1790 and 1810, the population of free black men and women grew at a rate

Frederick Douglass.
Library of Congress.

of more than eighteen times, to six thousand—more than double the rate of growth in New York.[51] However, the city retained a large slave population and was a key port in the transportation of slaves to places farther south, such as New Orleans. When the United States banned the international slave trade in 1808, the domestic trade worked to supply the southern states' need for human bondage, and Baltimore was a critical junction.

Frederick Douglass, the famous abolitionist, was one of those slaves sent to Baltimore. His owners on the Eastern Shore did not intend to sell him but to have him work with their relatives in the city, which was a fairly common situation. Many families earned money by renting out their slaves. The short-term cost of renting an individual slave was more affordable than the larger upfront cost of outright ownership, even if the long-term cost of renting was greater. Douglass described his thoughts about what it meant to him to move to Baltimore:

I shall never forget the ecstasy with which I received the intelligence that my old
master [Anthony] *had determined to let me go to Baltimore…If, however,*
I found in my new home hardship, hunger, whipping and nakedness, I had
the consolation that I should not have escaped any one of them by staying.[52]

Not surprisingly, his various times living in Baltimore proved difficult. He saw firsthand how having a slave changed a new mistress from a kind person to someone coldhearted, as well as how the competition for jobs between white men, free blacks and slaves created threatening circumstances for all involved. While working at William Gardiner's shipyards in Fells Point in 1836, Douglass was targeted by several white apprentices, who beat him up. "The fight was a desperate one, and I came out of it most shockingly mangled. I was cut and bruised in sundry places, and my left eye was nearly knocked out its socket."[53] However, it was while living in Baltimore that he learned to read and began questioning his life's situation.

As he acquired more knowledge, Douglass also acquired a stronger and stronger urge to be free. While living under William Freeland (but owned by Thomas Auld) in St. Michael's, Maryland, he hatched a plan to escape with

Arrival of Freedmen and Their Families at Baltimore, 1865. Library of Congress.

In April 1826, about thirty of Woolfolk's slaves were imprisoned aboard the *Decatur*, on its way to sell them in New Orleans. Included in the group was twenty-four-year-old William Bowser (also known as William Hill), who had belonged to the Harrison family in Baltimore County. While on board, he plotted a rebellion with the other slaves. On the fifth day of the voyage—somewhere off the coast of Georgia—the slaves mutinied. At least fifteen men, four boys, seven women and three girls participated in the uprising. Two of the men, Thomas Harrod and Manuel Wilson, threw Captain Walter R. Galloway overboard as he was scraping mud from the anchor stock. First mate William Porter soon followed. While the mutineers attempted to maneuver the boat toward Haiti, they lacked the training to sail the ship, and the remaining crew members were either not experienced or not willing to assist. The ship floundered for several days.

On May 2, the *Constitution*, a whaling vessel en route to Nantucket, overtook the ship and captured seventeen of the slaves, including eight women, two men and seven children, before continuing on its way. One crew member joined them. They left the remaining fourteen slaves on the ship, along with the crew members. Three days later, the *Rooke* encountered the *Decatur* and led it to New York. Once in port, all of the remaining slaves managed to escape. Only the leader of the insurrection, William Bowser, was caught. After being tried, he was found guilty and sentenced to hang. Apparently, someone with the name of Woolfolk was in the crowd when Bowser was hanged. Whether it was Austin or someone else is uncertain. According to reports, Bowser gave a small speech from the gallows, wherein he actually forgave Woolfolk for his wrongdoings and looked forward to seeing him in heaven. Woolfolk responded viciously, saying that Bowser "was now going to get what he deserved, and he was glad of it."

Back in Baltimore, Benjamin Lundy reported on the incident in his abolitionist newspaper, the *Genius of Universal Emancipation*. The paper, which also employed emerging advocate and abolitionist leader William Garrison, relayed what had occurred in New York, including the exchange between Bowser and Woolfolk. In response to the publication, Woolfolk accosted Lundy outside the post office. After confirming that he had published the article, Woolfolk "threw [Lundy] to the ground and beat and stamped upon his head and face in a most furious and violent manner until pulled off by the bystanders. Lundy was confined to his bed for several days."[60]

During the lawsuit that followed, Woolfolk admitted his fault and was found guilty, but he was only charged a single dollar as a fine. When the judge read the sentence, he included that "he had never seen a case in which the provocation for battery was greater than the present if abusive language could ever be a justification." He referred to the language of the article, which denounced slavery as "barbaric, inhuman, and unchristian" and referred to Woolfolk as a "soul seller."[61]

When Frederick Douglass was eventually released from prison, it was initially under the direction that he was to be shipped to Alabama. Thomas Auld eventually reconsidered and sent Douglass back to his brother Hugh Auld in Baltimore with the promise to emancipate him in a few years. Douglass worked as Hugh's slave for a while before finally running away. He borrowed a friend's pass, called a "sailor's protection," and took a train to New York, dressed in the part of a seaman. He wrote:

> *I had on a red shirt and a tarpaulin hat and black cravat, tied in sailor fashion, carelessly and loosely about my neck. My knowledge of ships and sailor's talk came much to my assistance, for I knew a ship from stern to stern, and from keelson to cross-trees, and could talk sailor like an 'old salt.'*[62]

When the conductor checked his papers, he persuaded the man that the pass, emblazoned with an eagle, was enough proof that he was a free man. The plot worked, and he made his way safely north. Douglass went on to become one of the most prominent speakers against slavery and worked to better the lives of all African Americans.

Meanwhile, Baltimore continued to serve as a major port for slave trading until the outbreak of the Civil War. In all, there are estimates of over a dozen slave traders operating in the city at the height of its trade, moving countless thousands of people throughout the country. However, the city was also a beacon—hosting several abolitionist newspapers, serving as home to many supporters of the Underground Railroad, providing networking opportunities for free blacks and slaves and offering a chance to run away to the North, which lay only a single state boundary away.

Would Poe Have Been Poe without Baltimore?

*I became first known to the literary world thus. A Baltimore weekly paper (*The Visiter*)*
offered two premiums—one for best prose story, one for best poem. The Committee
awarded both to me, and took occasion to insert in the journal a card, signed by
themselves, in which I was very highly flattered.
—Edgar Allan Poe, 1841

Baltimore's most morbid—and perhaps most famous—resident of all time was the famed writer of the macabre Edgar Allan Poe. Although he was not born in Baltimore, the city played an influential role in his life—and, of course, his death. Besides having deep familial ties to the city, Poe published his first story while here; met his future wife, Virginia, here (and may have even secretly married her here); and returned here to die a mysterious death that has all but cemented his status as a literary legend. Even in death, his story continues to be deeply enmeshed with the city that named its football team for his poem "The Raven," enshrined his home as a museum and waits every year at his grave site to see if the "Poe Toaster" will return.

Poe's connection to Baltimore begins with his paternal great-grandparents, John and Jane McBride Poe, who emigrated from Ireland and moved to the city around 1755. They brought several children in tow, including their eldest son, David, who would become Poe's grandfather. About ten years old when he arrived, David grew up in the city and, like many other Baltimoreans, was patriotic to the American cause. He spent

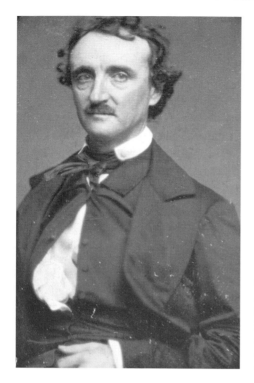

This photograph is potentially the last one that Edgar Allan Poe sat for, as it was taken approximately three weeks before his death. *The "Thompson Daguerreotype" of Edgar Allan Poe by William A. Pratt, 1849, Rare Book & Manuscript Library, Columbia University in the City of New York.*

40,000 silver dollars toward supplies for the Revolutionary War. His wife, Elizabeth, provided clothing to the Marquis de Lafayette's troops when they came through the city in 1781. Although commissioned as assistant deputy quartermaster general for the city, he never rose higher than the rank of major. A grateful citizenry dubbed him "General" for all of his and his family's many services.[63]

The couple had seven children, including Edgar's father, David, in 1784. As soon as he was of age, David left home to pursue an acting career, much against his father's wishes, and came back rarely. While on stage, he met actress Eliza (née Arnold) Hopkins. In 1806, about a year after the death of her first husband, the two married. She was only eighteen at the time. They had three children together, including Edgar, who was born in 1809 in Boston. His older brother, William Henry, came in 1807, and his younger sister, Rosalie, appeared in 1810.[64]

Edgar's early years were troubled. David abandoned the family sometime in 1811, and within the same year, Eliza died. The three children were split up and sent to different families. Edgar spent his formative years with the

Edgar Allan Poe House, Amity Street, Baltimore. *Author photograph.*

Allan family, although they were often turbulent. He and John Allan, the family patriarch, were regularly at odds with each other and eventually split ways. As a young man, Poe soon found his way back to his ancestral home.[65]

Around May 1831, he arrived in Baltimore and soon moved into his aunt Maria Clemm's tiny home on Mechanics Row, Wilks Street (today Eastern Avenue), alongside his grandmother Elizabeth; his brother, William Henry; his aunt's son, Henry; and her daughter, Virginia—a little girl of eight. The makeshift family struggled, as did Poe in his attempt to find work. He ended up writing several times to his estranged father for money but never received a response. Unfortunately, Poe's brother Henry did not survive the year, passing away on August 1 at the age of twenty-four.[66]

The year 1831 was also a turning point in Poe's career as a writer. Before moving to Baltimore, he had published his first set of poetry in *Poems by Edgar A. Poe.* Reviews appeared in the *New-York Mirror* and *Saturday Evening Post* shortly after he moved. While living in Baltimore, he submitted five stories to a contest held by the *Philadelphia Saturday Courier.* The *Courier* offered $100 for the best "American tale." While he didn't win the prize, the editors published all of his works over the course of the following year, including "Metzengerstein," "The Duke de L'Omelette," "A Tale of Jerusalem," "A Decided Loss" and "The Bargain Lost." Several of the works were reprinted in additional publications.[67]

While details of his life during this time are sketchy, he must have begun growing in literary stature, as evidenced by the following 1832 editorial in the *Baltimore Saturday Visiter*:

> *Mr. Edgar A. Poe, has favoured us with the perusal of some manuscript tales written by him. If we were merely to say that we had read them, it would be a compliment, for manuscripts of this kind are very seldom read by any one but the author. But we may further say that we have read these tales every syllable, with the greatest pleasure, and for originality, richness of imagery and purity of the style, few American authors in our opinion have produced any thing superior. With Mr. Poe's permission we may hereafter lay one or two of the tales before our readers.[68]*

During the following year, the *Saturday Visiter* announced a contest, which Poe readily entered. It included prizes for both prose and poetry. Poe was awarded the prize for prose for "Found in a Bottle." In fact, his entire submission—a series of stories loosely collected under the title "The Tales of the Folio Club"—received additional mention by the judges, who said:

> *Of the tales submitted there were many of various and distinguished excellence; but the singular force and beauty of those offered by The Tales of the Folio Club; it may be said without disparagement to the high merit of others presented in the competition, left us no ground for doubt in making choice of one from that collection…These tales are eminently distinguished by a wild, vigorous and poetical imagination, a rich style, a fertile invention, and varied and curious learning.*

Poe received a decent fifty dollars for the work.[69]

Although the judges were taken with Poe's work, he nonetheless lost the poetry prize to a piece entitled "The Song of the Winds." Supposedly written by Henry Wilton, Poe soon learned that it was actually composed by John Hill Hewitt, an editor for the *Saturday Visiter* and one of the competition judges. Upset by the dupe, he confronted Hewitt, who later wrote about the encounter:

[Poe] *approached me with an ominous scowl on his features.*

"You have used underhanded means, sir, to obtain that prize over me," *said he, sternly.*

"I deny it, sir;" was my reply.

"Then why did you keep back your real name?"

"I had my reasons, and you have no right to question me."

"But you tampered with the committee, sir."

"The committee are gentlemen above being tampered with, sir; and if you say that you insult them;" I replied, looking him full in the face.

"I agree that the committee are gentlemen," replied he, his dark eyes flashing with anger, "but I cannot place you in that category."

My blood mounted up to fever heat in a moment, and with my usual impulsiveness, I dealt him a blow which staggered him, for I was physically his superior.

There was every prospect of a very pretty fight, for Poe was full of pluck, but several gentlemen, friends to both parties, interfered, and the affair was "nipped in the bud:" There was no duel—much to the disappointment of our friends and well-wishers.[70]

In spite of the forsaken duel, the *Saturday Visiter* still advertised that it would publish the rest of Poe's tales, piling additional praise on the pieces. However, Poe, perhaps reeling from the sustained emotional punch of losing, declined the paper's wishes, wanting to unveil the stories in a Philadelphia-based publication.

Even as Poe was published in more and more locations, he nonetheless maintained financial difficulties. He made one more visit to Richmond to see his ailing foster father, John Allan, but was thrown out of the house. Allan died in March 1834. While he left nothing for Poe in his will, he did pass on portions of his fortune to all of his biological children, including several illegitimate ones.

In a strange turn of luck, Poe actually ended up moving to Richmond during the following year to begin working for the *Southern Literary Messenger*. By October, Maria Clemm and Virginia had joined him. He and Virginia were officially married in May 1836, but there are persistent rumors that the two may have secretly wed before ever leaving Baltimore. What is known is that while Poe never again lived in Baltimore, he somehow managed to die there.[71]

How many ways can a person die? At last count, over a dozen theories exist on what took Poe's life. He stopped in Baltimore on September 28, 1849, on his way to New York City from Richmond. Additional details about his remaining days are murky at best. On October 3, Joseph W. Walker discovered Poe "in great distress" at Ryan's 4th Ward Polls, a tavern located on Lombard Street. The famed writer was delirious and wearing ill-fitting, strange clothes. Walker notified one of Poe's friends, Dr. J.E. Snodgrass, who helped collect the unfortunate Poe. They notified relatives in the area and took him to Washington College Hospital. After four difficult days, he died on October 7 at the age of forty. According to his attending physician, Dr. John J. Moran, Poe's last words were: "Lord help my poor soul."[72]

What took Poe's life? Unfortunately, there are no surviving death certificates. According to the contemporaneous newspaper the *Baltimore Clipper*, he died of "congestion of the brain." This somewhat vague description gives little to go on, but several additional theories have been promulgated, including complicated murder conspiracies, depression leading to suicide and more.[73]

During the mid-nineteenth century, Baltimore was overrun with corruption, which often led to violence in the streets. Political gangs (which will be discussed in detail in a later chapter) would force unwitting victims into drinking, voting, changing their clothing and then voting again and again at the same polling site. These gangs might beat their victims into submission. This practice was known as "cooping" for the little rooms—or coops—where the gangs kept their victims. Notably, Poe was found on election day outside Ryan's Tavern, which served as a voting site. A normally fashionable dresser, his clothes were definitely not his own. According to Dr. Moran, his clothing included "a stained, faded, old bombazine coat, pantaloons of a similar character, a pair of worn-out shoes run down at the heels, and an old straw hat." Would Poe's fame have saved him from being considered for this scam, which required victims to appear inconspicuous?[74]

Several diseases have been fingered as potential culprits: brain tumor, syphilis, heart disease, tuberculosis, epilepsy, diabetes and cholera. Dr. R. Michael Benitez, a cardiologist at the University of Maryland Medical Center (UMMC), postulated that Poe may have died of rabies. In a 1996 UMMC report, he suggested that Poe may have contracted the disease from a bite from a rabid animal, perhaps even one of his own pets. The report says, "In the final stages of rabies, it is common for people to have periods of confusion that come and go, along with wide swings in pulse rate and other body functions, such as respiration and temperature." These symptoms fit the description of Poe's final days at Washington College Hospital. Furthermore, people normally only survive for four days when faced with such an extreme case of rabies—the exact amount of time that Poe was in the hospital before dying. One of the major symptoms to support Benitez's rabies claim—hydrophobia, or a fear of water—has been reputed by an 1875 text reporting that Poe had no difficulty swallowing water.[75]

Some have argued whether metal poisoning could have done in Poe. In 2006, the Edgar Allan Poe Society released a report that tested locks of his hair. While traces of arsenic, lead, mercury, nickel, uranium and vanadium were present, none was in high enough amounts to indicate poisoning.[76]

What about Poe's infamous identity as a notorious drunk? Medical records suggest that Poe refused alcohol in the hospital. While he had recently joined the Sons of Temperance, some historians believe this was simply a ploy to win over Elmira Shelton. A widow living in Richmond, Shelton and Poe had been infatuated with each other when younger. Her father surreptitiously intercepted the letters they wrote to each other until they were both convinced the other had forsaken them. Each went on to marry someone else and outlive their spouses. When Poe returned to Richmond in the summer of 1849, he resumed courting Shelton and asked for her hand in marriage. While it is unclear whether they were formally engaged (Shelton later denied that they were), there are reports that they were set to be married on October 17.

Nonetheless, there are two contemporary reports suggesting that Poe did indulge in drink to excess. However, like so many other accounts, they cannot be taken on face value alone.

When Joseph Walker found Poe outside Ryan's Tavern, he sent a letter to Snodgrass, who assumed Poe's illness was nothing more than severe intoxication. Snodgrass, an adamant teetotaler, published claims that Poe died from alcoholism. However, his various reports tended to change and contradict one another over the years. Additionally, Dr. Moran, Poe's attending physician, claimed, "I have stated to you the fact that Edgar Allan Poe did not die under the effect of any intoxicant, nor was the smell of liquor upon his breath or person."[77]

Rufus Griswold and Poe had worked together before a falling out caused them to become bitter rivals. After Poe died, he wrote an obituary under the pseudonym Ludwig, which called Poe "brilliant but erratic." Then,

Griswold went so far as to position himself as Poe's literary executor and used his power to write a demeaning biography of Poe, which depicted him as little more than a depraved, heavy-drinking madman.[78]

In *Midnight Dreary*, John Evangelist Walsh provides a remarkably complex tale leading to Poe's untimely demise. He suggests that Shelton's brothers, unhappy with the coupling, followed him on his trip north, making it all the way to Philadelphia. They demanded that he remain in New York and call off his engagement to their sister. Walsh believes that Poe next sought refuge with his friend John Sartain.[79] In later years, Sartain wrote about a strange incident involving Poe, which he had dated to earlier that summer:

> *The last time I saw Mr. Poe was late in that same year, 1849, and then under such peculiar and almost fearful conditions that the experience can never fade from my memory. Early one Monday afternoon he suddenly entered into my engraving room, looking pale and haggard, with a wild and frightened expression in his eyes…"Mr. Sartain, I have come to you for a refuge and protection; will you let me stay with you? It is necessary to my safety that I lie concealed for a time." I assured him that he was welcome, that in my house he would be perfectly safe, and he could stay as long as he liked, but I asked him what was the matter. He said it would be difficult for me to believe what he had to tell, or that such things were possible in this nineteenth century…After he had had time to calm down a little, he told me that he had been on his way to New York, but he had overheard some men who sat a few seats back of him plotting how they should kill him and then throw him off from the platform of the car. He said they spoke so low that it would have been impossible for him to hear and understand the meaning of their words, had it not been that his sense of hearing was so wonderfully acute. They could not guess that he heard them, as he sat so quiet and apparently indifferent to what was going on, but when the train arrived at the Bordentown station he gave them the slip and remained concealed until the cars moved on again. He had returned to Philadelphia by the first train back, and hurried to me for refuge.[80]*

While Sartain doubted Poe's story, he nonetheless followed along and asked why they would trouble him. Poe responded that it was "for revenge" over "a woman trouble." Sartain did not intrude further, but Walsh believes that this was an allusion to Elmira Shelton. The incident became even stranger, as

Poe suddenly asked for Sartain's assistance with shaving off his moustache, so as to disguise himself from his pursuers. Sartain writes, "I told him that as I never shaved I had no razor, but if he wanted it removed I could readily do it for him with scissors. Accordingly I took him to the bathroom and performed the operation successfully."[81] Walsh suggests that this attempt at disguise may explain why Poe was found in strange clothing. He points out that no one includes in their description of Poe whether or not he had a moustache, whereas reports and photographs from earlier in the summer include one.

Walsh concludes that Poe headed back to Richmond not long after his encounter with Sartain, only to be found by the brothers in Baltimore. He says that they may have beaten him so badly and filled him with so much whiskey that it eventually led to his death.[82]

A recent theory by Michael Powell contends that Poe did not disappear at all. He says that the notion that Poe was lost around Baltimore came from Shelton, when she talked carelessly with Maria Clemm. Powell believes Poe was found ill while on a train en route to Philadelphia and was taken back to Baltimore to be cared for by his family and friends there. He argues that this would have put Poe in Baltimore only hours before he was discovered outside Ryan's 4th Ward Tavern. Nor does he think that Moran ever treated Poe; he suggests the doctor only discovered that the patient was in his hospital after he died and tried to take advantage of the opportunity it presented.[83]

While Poe's remaining days and strange condition remain shrouded in mystery, Jeff Jerome, curator of the Poe House in Baltimore, provides a far more straightforward reason for the writer's death. He believes that what killed Poe was the same thing intended to save him: medical treatment. While reports indicated that Poe refused alcohol in the hospital, did that include refusing laudanum, an opium and alcohol tincture regularly used to treat a variety of ailments? Perhaps the use of this drug may explain why Poe would go in and out of lucidity during his visit; every time he appeared to be getting better, the medical staff would give him another dosage, sending him spiraling out again. This may explain why Neilson Poe, the writer's cousin, was surprised that Poe died after seeing him doing better only the day before. Could his death be attributed to an unintended overdose?

Even in death, Poe cannot lie peacefully. Since being moved in 1875 into a grave site with a more elaborate monument at Westminster Hall, historians have debated whether the correct person was identified. Charles Scarlett believes that instead of Poe, gravediggers actually exhumed Philip Mosher

Edgar Allan Poe's grave site at Westminster Hall. *Author photograph.*

Jr., a War of 1812 soldier whose family lot lies next to Poe's.[84] However, Christopher Scharpf argued that this misconception was due to a series of incorrect statements and misunderstandings. According to his research, the correct people are in the correct places.[85]

Additionally, Poe's body is currently the subject of a feud between Baltimore and Philadelphia. In 2008, scholar Edward Petit argued that Poe's body should be moved to Philadelphia because "his greatest stories are written [there]."[86] Poe's Philadelphia stories include "The Fall of the House of Usher," "The Murders in the Rue Morgue," "The Masque of the Red Death," "The Tell-Tale Heart," "The Black Cat" and "The Gold-Bug."

Jeff Jerome argued in response, "We have his body. And no body snatcher from Philadelphia or any other city is going to come here in the middle of the night and steal away his body." He pointed out that Baltimore was the first place to respect Poe's talents and that his first true horror story, "Berenice," was written while he lived in Baltimore during the 1830s. While the battle wages on, Poe's remains remain lying in wait.[87]

Baltimore continues to be obsessed with Poe's death. Every year since 1949, a mysterious figure in black with a wide-brimmed hat and white scarf has made a pilgrimage to Poe's grave on the author's birthday, January 19. The unknown person always leaves three roses and a partially filled bottle of cognac. Several have claimed to be the famous "Poe Toaster," but none of the claims has been substantiated. In 2010 and 2011, the Poe Toaster did not appear, leaving the city to wonder if yet another strange death had occurred.

Plug Uglies, Blood Tubs
and Rip Raps, Oh My!

Maryland is often a strange, paradoxical place. Although the initial colony was founded as a Catholic safe haven, it soon became one of the most bigoted, vicious places for Catholics to reside. In 1649, the state legislature passed the Toleration Act, which attempted to bridge relations between Catholics and Protestants, but it was repealed a mere five years later. Even after becoming a state and consecrating the first American cathedral in 1821, anti-Catholic sentiment loomed in great measure. This fervor erupted in 1839 in what is known as the Nunnery Riot. On August 18, a young woman named Isabella "Sarah" Neale escaped from the Carmelite nunnery on Aisquith Street. She ran down the street in full religious garb, knocking on doors until Mr. Wilcox, a deputy warden, gave her refuge.

The *Sun* reported that her family had long considered her mentally unstable, as she had been

> *exhibiting symptoms of insanity, a malady that her brother is now laboring under, and after admission to the convent the evidences of an alienation of reason became stronger and stronger, until she became so eccentric that at the advice of the physician of the institution she was withdrawn from the school-room and allowed to indulge in the solitude she seemed desirous to court.*

While at the nunnery, she had stopped eating, save "peach leaves, grass, and other articles not edible for a human being." At one meal, she pretended to resume interest in food and, while in the kitchen, leaped through the window to escape.[88]

Word of the strange incident spread quickly, and people started crowding the area. Concerned about a riot breaking out, Mayor S.C. Leakin came and resolved that Neale would be escorted to Washington Medical College.[89] He called in reinforcements, which quelled the impending violence, although tempers simmered throughout the next day. The convent allowed outsiders to tour the facility, attempting to prove that no one had been held there against her will. Still, imaginations were fired up by the incident.[90]

Anti-Catholic sentiment festered throughout the city, fueled by additional religious attacks in the media. Nor was the feeling limited to Catholics. Immigrants of all religious backgrounds and countries were pouring into the city, which on the whole was becoming larger and more diverse. Many residents saw these newcomers not only as different and undesirable but also as competition—both for jobs in a struggling economy and as potential players in an increasingly sophisticated political arena. In short, Baltimore was entering its adolescent years, where its leaders tried different methods to accommodate changes in its infrastructure and the needs of its growing population.

All of these disparate fears helped feed the popularity of the emerging American Party, which was gaining steam out of the dissipating Whig party. The Americans were a right-wing, nativist political umbrella organization, which included several smaller violent gangs, loosely organized as the Know-Nothings. They were called Know-Nothings because members answered that they "knew nothing" when questioned by authorities regarding their aggressive activities. The Know-Nothings were particularly strong in Baltimore, where they included groups in the majority of wards with such unusual and colorful names as the Blood Tubs, McGonigan's Rip Raps, Natives, Rough Skins, Tigers, Black Snakes, Wampanoags, Regulators, Double-Pumps, Hunters, American Rattlers, Butt Enders, Blackguards and so on.[91]

"Gangs of young men parade public thoroughfares, armed with knives and revolvers," wrote the *Sun* in 1857, describing the makeup of these groups, which relied on violence and intimidation. "Collisions have been frequent between Americans and citizens of Irish and German extraction. The most bitter hostility has been encouraged between native and foreign-born citizens."[92]

Know Nothing Polka, by James
Couenhaven, 1854. *Library of Congress.*

Perhaps the most notorious gang of Know-Nothings in Baltimore was called
the Plug Uglies. In 1857, the *Washington Star* called it "as pestilent and scrofulous
a brood of scoundrels as hell itself could vomit from its vilest crater."[93] Growing
out of the Mount Vernon Hook-and-Ladder Company—an all-volunteer
firefighting group—the Plug Uglies were nasty, contemptible political gangsters
who generally ran with McGonigan's Rip Raps and often tangled with any
Democrats in the city. According to folklore, the name "Plug Ugly" possibly
refers to a specific gang member who was considered ugly to look upon but
generous with his tobacco plugs—an inverse of the expression "ugly plug" or
the "ugly blows" the gang delivered in its fights.[94] Eventually, the term would be
linked to anyone who was considered a "rowdy."

Members took pride in their brutal actions, even composing songs about
their "valor" and strength. One such ditty was entitled "The Plug Uglies!"
The song praises the gang's ability to help elect or run out particular political
candidates, including mayoral candidates, as well as former president Millard

The Morning after the Election, November 1856, by John Childs and John Magee. *Sterns Collection, Library of Congress.*

Fillmore, who ran an unsuccessful reelection campaign in 1856 as the American Party candidate. During the election, he only carried Maryland. Part of the song goes as follows:

> *We are a gallant band of spirits, fair or foul,*
> *Who glory in our valor and firmness of our soul,*
> *Our watch-word is "now go it," so we'll ever cry,*
> *Oh! you Plug Uglies, now root hog or die.*
>
> *For we are the native party in the west end who try,*
> *Go it Plug and Uglies, root 'em out or die.*
>
> *We don't like the Demmy's, for Fillmore is our boast,*
> *And here in old Maryland he is a perfect host,*
> *Nor do we love the Argus, with all its boasted eyes,*
> *For our motto is "ever on," root hog or die.*
>   *For we are the native party…*
>
> *But as we are all natives; and proudly we can brag,*
> *As true sons of America, we'll fight beneath its flag,*

Nor from the field of honor, never will we fly,
But as good Plug Uglies we'll root hog or die.
For we are the native party...[95]

Although it may sound strange today to hear of a firefighting company described as violent, members of the Plug Uglies' Mount Vernon Hook-and-Ladder Company were just as likely to get into a fight with a rival company, like the New Market Firemen, as they were to actually extinguish a fire. As fires raged and threatened surrounding buildings, the firefighters would regularly ignore their duties to engage in "battle royals" with one another, using their axes, picks, hooks and even the street cobblestones and sidewalk bricks.[96] In fact, some of the members, such as the perennially arrested and released John Wesley Gambrill, were accused of starting several fires.[97]

Vigilant Fire Company fireman, Baltimore, circa 1840–60. *Marian S. Carson Collection, Library of Congress.*

The Know-Nothings were soon deeply enmeshed in all aspects of city life. Oftentimes, several well-to-do businessmen would start a fire company, while working-class men, such as tavern keepers and coopers, would run a corresponding gang. Several Know-Nothing members also belonged to the corrupted local police force. Some even infiltrated the judicial system, whether serving as lawyers, clerks or possibly even as judges. All together, they used their influence—whether financial or violent in nature—to elect American Party members to all the branches of city and state government, including mayors and governors.

Election day typically brought about the worst violence. Unlike today, voting was a public act. A voter would carry brightly colored and sometimes patterned ballots to his designated ward house, such as a local saloon. If a Know-Nothing found a voter carrying the "wrong" ballot, the voter might be whipped, beaten or worse. The Blood Tubs, for example, drew their name because of their propensity to dunk their victims in buckets of pigs' blood and refuse.[98] Occasionally, people were even killed.

On October 8, 1856, rioting overtook the city as the municipal elections were held. Two former railroad presidents, the American Thomas Swann of the Baltimore & Ohio Railroad and the Democrat Robert Clinton Wright of the Baltimore & Susquehanna Railroad, vied for the position of mayor. Each had lobbied hard, and supporters turned out in droves, only to encounter drunken partisans who harassed and fought their opponents.

Tensions mounted as the day continued. In the early afternoon, a group of Plug Uglies and their Rip Rap friends encountered a group of New Market firemen near Lexington Market. Fighting broke out between the respective American and Democrat groups. Instead of using bricks and picks, this time the gangs came armed with muskets, shotguns and blunderbusses. They even rolled in a cannon. Like an old movie western showdown, people fled the area as neighborhood residents locked up their homes and businesses. The *Sun* reported that the encounter went "unchecked and unherded, apparently, by any show of police force." The battle raged in "guerilla fashion" for over three hours, killing Charles Brown and James Rodgers. Brown took a shot to the chest, while another shot sliced open Rodgers' neck artery.

Others were seriously wounded, including the Democrat Henry Konig, who caught a ball in his thigh, while another passed through American Boney Lee's side and back. American Guy Silwright took three shots. Somehow, all three men managed to survive.[99] One man named Feaster had a ball extracted from his leg at a local doctor's office. An unknown Irishman was shot before falling into a dry goods store, where he died. Another man received a shot through his head, passing through his upper jawbone. Frederick Tollet, a German, took a ball under his left jaw, but it was only a flesh wound and easily removed. Thomas Morrison was shot in the leg. Martin Wooden was shot in the groin. The *Sun* remarked that the wound was "painful but not dangerous."[100]

By early evening, the Americans had won the battle, which culminated in the group breaking off the doors of the New Market engine house. The *Sun* estimated that there were "perhaps some two hundred shots fired during this protracted warfare."

The rioting continued elsewhere—with different results. In the Eighth Ward, another group of Plug Uglies fought with a gang of Democrats. During the confrontation, several people were killed. A teenager from D.C. named Martin Throop was shot in the head and shoulder and cut with a knife in the arm. Although his brain protruded from the wound, he managed to survive for five days before dying. Daniel Broderick was shot and lingered for almost a month before finally dying. A Plug Ugly named Carter and Democrat Patrick Dunleavy were both killed. Unlike at the New Market engine house, the Democrats were the larger force here, sending the Plug Uglies into retreat. In other wards, serious incidents occurred—and the fighting continued for days—but no other full-scale riots happened.[101]

In the end, American Thomas Swann carried the election, beating the Democrat Wright by 1,551 votes. Interestingly, for all his violent connections, Swann went on to become a largely progressive mayor, establishing the first streetcars and developing several city parks, including Druid Hill Park. He was reelected in 1858 after the newly developed City Reform Association's candidate, Colonel A.P. Shutt, bowed out in the middle of election day itself.

All of the violence meted out thus far was simply a prelude of what was to come. During the November presidential elections, former president Millard Fillmore, running as the American Party candidate, went up against Democrat James Buchanan. The current mayor, Samuel Hinks, wavered on whether to bring in military force to police the election. Governor T. Watkins Ligon, a Democrat, argued in favor of the plan, but Hinks ultimately decided against it, determining that the municipal police would be enough.

Election day began much like the previous one had with small fights, growing anger and lots of drinking. By mid-afternoon, the fighting grew larger and more organized as Americans and Democrats again turned the city into their personal battlefield. Over a dozen people were killed, while more than 100 (some estimate 250) were wounded, including women and children. Mayor Hinks had been horribly mistaken. The police force was overwhelmed by the violence, with several members actively engaged in instigating it. In stark contrast to Baltimore's fatalities, the *Sun* reported that in New York, there was some "fighting in the course of the forenoon in the course of which pistols and firearms were freely used, resulting in a plentiful crop of black eyes and bloody noses, but nothing more serious."[102]

Fillmore won the state by more than seven thousand votes but fell short throughout the rest of the country. The American party was pro-Union, unlike the Democrats, who favored states' rights. Meanwhile, in the more northern states, the Republican Party was growing at a feverish pace, replacing many American loyalties. While the American Party was being quickly dismantled on the national scale, it managed to retain its hold in Baltimore for several years, where the city's long history of patriotism at all costs helped secure American sympathies.

Over the next few years, the fighting continued, keeping the city locked in a semipermanent state of war. Everything came to a head in the 1859 elections. Sick of the endless, constantly escalating violence, the city's public began fighting back. On September 8, a large group of Baltimoreans gathered in Monument Square to "devise some means of rescuing our city from its present deplorable condition." They drafted a number of "reform bills," such as taking control of the police away from municipal government. A committee was organized with the valiant attempt to secure nominations of honorable men for elected positions, "without regard to party, and to be selected from the best, most reliable, and most competent men in this community."[103]

Meanwhile, the Know-Nothings held a counter-demonstration. They held up placards with a picture of a shoemaker's awl and a caption reading, "With this we will do our work." They even brought a blacksmith who forged awls on-site for participants.[104]

Mayor Swann refused to work with the reform association. He stood behind his administration and claimed:

> *I do not hesitate to say that the press has done more injury to this city than ten times the catalogue of rowdyism which it has professed to detail. It has*

excited your people to riot and blood-shed at home, and has brought discredit upon your good name abroad…If you go to other communities similarly situated as our own—with the same mixed population—you will find that rowdyism is not more remarkable in this city than in some of these.[105]

While the association failed to achieve all its objectives during the October election, it managed to accomplish more than any other previous attempt, including acquiring seven seats in the new First Branch of the city council. Unsurprisingly, election day was not without incident. Reform challengers and Know-Nothings knocked at one another all day. In the Twentieth Ward, men broke into the ward house and destroyed the ballots. However, their candidate, Henry Placide, disapproved of their actions and conceded.

At the November election, violence again continued to reign supreme. George H. Kyle was one of many who submitted testimony to the Maryland House of Delegates about his experiences that day:

I went to the polls about half-past 8 A.M. and was within two feet of the window; remained there about five minutes with my brother [Adam B. Kyle]. I had a bundle of tickets under my arm, and one of the men walked up to me and asked me what it was that I had. I told him tickets; he made a snatch at them, and I avoided him and turned around. As I turned I heard my brother say: "I am struck, George!"

At that moment, I was struck from behind a severe blow on the back of my head, which would have knocked me down, but the crowd which had gathered around us was so dense that I was, as it were, kept up. After I received this blow I drew a dirk knife which I had in my pocket, with which I endeavored to strike the man, who, as I supposed, had struck me.

I then felt a pistol placed right close to my head, so that I felt the cold steel upon my forehead. At that moment I made a little motion to turn my head, which caused the shot of the pistol to glance from my head; my hat showed afterwards the mark of a bullet which I supposed to have been from that shot.

The discharge of the pistol, which blew off a large piece of skin of my forehead and covered my face with blood, caused me to fall. When I arose I saw my brother in the middle of the street, about ten feet from me, surrounded by a crowd who were striking at him and firing pistols all round him. He was knocked down twice, and at one time while he was down, I saw two men jump on his body and kick him…

In the meantime I drew my pistol and fired into the crowd, which was immediately in front of me, every man of whom seemed to have a pistol in his hand and was firing as rapidly as he could; in this crowd there were fully from forty to fifty persons.

I saw at the second story windows of the Watchman engine-house building, in which the polls were held, cut-off muskets or large pistols protruding, and observed smoke issuing from the muzzles, as though they were being fired at me; then I turned toward my brother and endeavored to get to him.

When within a few feet of him, I saw him fall...At the same moment a shot struck me in the shoulder, which went through my arm and penetrated my breast; from the direction the ball took I am satisfied that shot was fired from the second story of the engine house...

As I continued to back off a brick struck me in the breast and I fell... The crowd was firing at me constantly. When I arose...there were seven bullet holes in my coat and my coat was cut as if by knives in various places; the pantaloons also had the appearance of having been cut by bullets.

During all this time I saw no police officers...

My brother died that evening from the effect of the injuries received there.[106]

Between the violence and accusations of voting fraud, the Maryland state legislature decided that the election was illegitimate. It disbanded the old police force and developed a new one under state control. The reforms continued on the municipal level as well. The volunteer fire companies had already been dismantled and replaced with a new paid system "under the direct management and control of the municipal authorities"—an ordinance that Swann supported. In February 1859, the Baltimore City Fire Department had begun operation, immediately ending the rival company clashes and reducing the number of fires started on purpose by those companies.[107] As a result of the changes, a Reform mayor and city council were elected on a remarkably peaceful day in 1860. The age of the Know-Nothing Party had ended.

Political violence did not disappear in one fell swoop, hanging on for several decades. During the presidential campaign in 1868, Republican candidates Ulysses S. Grant and Schuyler Colfax were matched against Democrats Horatio Seymour and Francis Blair. In an article for *Frank Leslie's Illustrated*

Newspaper, a *Washington Evening Star* reporter recounted his experience coming through Baltimore on board a train bound for Philadelphia, where he encountered "one of the most villainous and cut-throat looking mobs that ever disgraced even Baltimore."

The train first stopped briefly at Annapolis Junction, where a young man came on board and took a poll of who the men planned to support in the election. The reporter said that the boy "reported fifty votes for Seymour and Blair, forty-two for Grant and Colfax, and seven neutral or who declined." Unbeknownst to the passengers, the information was transmitted ahead of the train to Baltimore in an attempt to "spot the Republicans."

Since many of those voting for Seymour and Blair were Baltimoreans, they got off the train when it stopped at Camden Station (today Camden Yards). The remaining passengers were primarily Republicans en route to Philadelphia. After the train's three cars were decoupled, they were attached to horses to be taken across Pratt Street to President Street Station. The reporter described the terrifying incident that happened next:

> [The first car was] *halted on the east side of President Street depot,* [where] *it was almost instantly taken possession of by a mob of roughs, upward of a hundred in number, who leaped upon the front and rear platforms, and occupied both doors of exit, so as to make sure of the passengers inside. The mob crowded against the windows, shouting for Seymour and Blair, which was their rallying cry. Then they flocked into the car and filled the passageway between the seats till it was impossible for the passengers to escape. The ruffians inside commenced an examination of each passenger. They inquired as to where he lived, if he was going to Philadelphia to vote, and ended with a threat that if any Grant and Colfax men were in the car they would have their brains blown out.*
>
> *A party of three or four accosted William Thorton, a Philadelphian, and assistant surveyor at the Metropolitan Hotel, Washington, who was sitting quietly in his seat, in this wise: The leader presented a cocked revolver, which he held directly against Thornton's mouth, saying, "Where do you live? Are you going to Philadelphia to vote? Tell me quick, or I'll blow your brains out!" adding a horrible oath. Thornton begged them to spare his life, and to mollify them, told them that he was one of Billy McMullen's crowd in Philadelphia. The man with the pistol said, "You lie. I believe you are one of the Radicals going to Philadelphia to vote; and if I thought you were,*

I would kill you right here." He added, in a threatening manner, "Who do you know in Philadelphia that can vouch for you? Tell me somebody I know in Philadelphia, or I will kill you," still holding the pistol to his face. Thornton held up his hands and swore that he was telling the truth, when the ruffian left him, begging him to excuse them for having treated one of McMullen's crowd so roughly. A colored man, who sat in the rear of Mr. Thornton, was next assailed with black jacks over the head by three or four of the ruffians for daring to look at them. He gave no provocation whatever.

While this was going on inside, the crowd outside was incessantly yelling, "Bring them out. Kill every one of them! Don't let one of them go on the train! Throw them under the cars!" The other passengers expected every moment to have their turn of cross-examination in the same style as that administered to Mr. Thornton, but before the examiners had time to go through the entire car in this way, the next one arrived, when the mob ran down toward it and beat several of the passengers in the most brutal manner. One passenger was pulled bodily out of the side window and kicked and beaten by the mob till they could pummel him no more. The third car arrived, and its occupants were treated in the same way; and after this, the ruffians staggered through the cars, shouting for Seymour and Blair, with imprecations that if any Grant and Colfax man dared to say he was for either of them, they would kill him on the spot. None of the passengers were armed, at least no weapons were displayed by them.[108]

The reporter then went on to describe an oddly comical incident. One of the assailants accused the passengers of cutting his head, and he threatened to shoot whoever had done it. Someone responded that it was a man in a light coat. The assailant grabbed a man matching the description. Before he could shoot him, someone else cried out, "That's not the man; he's in the last car." The ruffian and his entourage rushed down to the rear car, but by this time, the train had started backing up. As the train continued down Canton Avenue, the mob followed it, but the violence had ended. The reporter noted that during the entire incident, he noticed that "there were three or four uniformed policemen present, who appeared either to fraternize with the rioters, or to be afraid of them, for no arrests were made, as could be seen from the cars."[109]

Not surprisingly, Seymour and Blair won Maryland, along with seven additional states. However, they were no match for Grant and Colfax, who carried twenty-six states and won the election.

The Baltimore Plot

Baltimore and the Beginning of the Civil War

W as someone really going to murder the incoming president? Detective Allan Pinkerton wasn't hired to look into this concern. Surely, he must have thought that Abraham Lincoln had other people looking into these matters. However, Pinkerton didn't see them in Baltimore during the winter of 1861. And he was getting to know this city since he had arrived from Chicago. He and his operatives were investigating the possibility of an attack on the Philadelphia, Wilmington & Baltimore Railroad on behalf of its president, Samuel M. Felton. The soon-to-be president's train—the Lincoln Special—was due into Baltimore on February 23. Pinkerton couldn't help wondering: Would secessionists prevent his train from arriving—or worse, destroy the train with Lincoln and his family on board? Would they wait until the president arrived in the city and assassinate him here? If such a conspiracy existed, Pinkerton realized that it was far more important than the worries of one railroad baron. He needed to find out, and if it proved true, he needed to alert Lincoln soon.

Baltimore hated Abraham Lincoln. There was no doubt about that. Most of the citizens regularly bickered with one another over political matters, often rioting for and against various candidates. However, most of them agreed on how much they despised Lincoln. He only received 2 percent of the vote—just over one thousand votes—in the city and may have fared even worse if the Democrats were not already so deeply divided. When elected on November 7, 1860, a local newspaper wrote, "We cannot offer to the readers of The *Sun* one word of congratulations upon so inauspicious a result."[110]

Abraham Lincoln. *Harris & Ewing Collection, Library of Congress.*

While there were some Republicans in the city, they were a meager minority. The group had seen its rallying marches—referred to as "Wide Awakes"—ridiculed and stormed by the larger Know-Nothing and Democrat groups. They were ready to invite Lincoln to Baltimore, but the mayor and governor were less forthcoming with formal invitations, which was in stark contrast to the other cities where Lincoln had been overloaded with events in his honor.

Even in the face of an unfriendly welcome, Lincoln was determined to come to Baltimore. Although the city was known as "Mobtown," it was still in America. Also, it was the only stop on his two-week journey south of the Mason-Dixon line and the only state he'd visit where slavery was legal. How would Baltimore—and the rest of the country—see him if he ignored it? The country was ripping at the seams, and it needed a strong, resolute leader, not a whimpering coward.

Pinkerton saw things differently. If Lincoln stopped in Baltimore, the great parade of people coming to see him could easily hide a murderer in its wings. Even in Buffalo, New York, Lincoln had been nearly trampled to death by the friendly crowd waiting to see him. He didn't have any real security detail save one friend—Ward Hill Lamon—who acted in the role of bodyguard, and his movements were printed regularly in newspapers. It would be easy to attack—and possibly kill—him. If that happened, things would be much worse than just being called a coward. Without a doubt, a war would break out.

Pinkerton and his operatives—including America's first female detective, Kate Warne—discovered several potential plots afoot in Baltimore. While pretending to be John H. Hutchinson, a stockbroker in the Howard House hotel downtown, his contacts would meet with him privately, relaying what they had learned. All of them went undercover, meeting with people suspected of being rabid secessionists who might be planning to hurt Lincoln or would know who might be.

While the group investigated several people, much of Pinkerton's attention became focused on Captain Cipriano Ferrandini, an Italian American who was a barber at Barnum's Hotel, the "favorite resort of the Southern Element."[111] The hotel was located on the southwest corner of Monument Square at Fayette and Calvert Streets. He was the president of a secret society called the National Volunteers that was devoted to the Southern cause. One of Pinkerton's operatives—operating under the pseudonym of Joseph Howard—attended a meeting where Ferrandini gave a fiery speech, advocating that "this hireling Lincoln shall never, never be President. My life is of no consequence in a cause like this, and I am willing to give it for his. As Orsini gave his life for Italy, I am ready to die for the rights of the South and to crush out the abolitionist."[112] Howard managed to introduce Pinkerton to Ferrandini, pretending that he was from Georgia and that his sympathies were with the South. In this guise, Pinkerton and Howard interviewed Ferrandini, learning that there were plans already in place to assassinate Lincoln when he arrived in town. According to him, even the chief of police Marshal George Kane was warm to the plan and accepting of the outcome.

The two men soon changed their attention to one of Ferrandini's men: Lieutenant Otis K. Hillard, a member of the Palmetto Guards, a secret military organization in the city. Howard and Hillard became good friends, and Hillard soon relayed the particulars of the plot itself. He said that a "vast crowd" would meet Lincoln at the Calvert Street depot when his train arrived. Since laws from the 1830s prevented trains from connecting through the downtown, he would take an open carriage to the Camden Street depot. In Pinkerton's memoir, he elaborated on what Hillard said was planned next:

Here it was arranged that but a small force of policemen should be stationed, and as the President arrived a disturbance would be created which would attract the attention of these guardians of the peace, and this accomplished, it would be an easy task for a determined man to shoot the President, and, aided by his companions, succeed in making his escape.[113]

Hillard went on to say that conspirators were already in place in other cities, watching what Lincoln's party was doing and "ready to telegraph to Baltimore any change of route or delay in arrival." They had even worked out a cipher to encrypt their messages. The only item left to determine was which one of the men would actually murder Lincoln. A ballot would be used to figure out who take on the role.[114]

Another Pinkerton operative, Timothy Webster, had been sent to Perrymansville and went undercover in a Rebel company. After drilling one morning, the captain of the group took Webster into his confidence, where he was introduced to three men from a "secret league from Baltimore."[115] The group decided not only that they would assassinate Lincoln, but also that they would destroy telegraph wires and burn railroad bridges to keep the Northern states from rising up against Maryland.

Meanwhile, two other groups were researching the same problem. William Seward—the soon-to-be secretary of state—had come to the same conclusion as Pinkerton. Additionally, New York City police detective David S. Bookstaver, working for Colonel Charles P. Stone, went undercover in unveiling the plot with some success. Stone considered Bookstaver's information as being "entirely corroborative of that already in our possession."[116]

A congressionally appointed group called the Select Committee of Five had started investigating the threat in January and even interviewed several of the same men whom Pinkerton and the other groups examined, including Ferrandini. They learned from Ferrandini that he had become a captain while training in Mexico and taught "infantry tactics" while in Maryland. He frankly asserted that the National Volunteers had been "formerly a political association" but was now "drilling as a military volunteer corps." He claimed that the group didn't have arms or an armory and that it had no intention of disrupting the inauguration. "They are formed for this purpose," said Ferrandini, "to prevent northern volunteer companies from passing through the State of Maryland." Even with these ostentatious claims, the Select Committee of Five nonetheless determined that the evidence was insubstantial and that the threat was not real:

> *The committee are unanimously of the opinion that the evidence produced before them does not prove the existence of a secret organization here or elsewhere hostile to the government, that has for its object, upon its own responsibility, an attack upon the Capitol, or any of the public property here, or an interruption of any of the functions of the government.*[117]

Still, Pinkerton felt he and his operatives had collected enough evidence. He decided that the threat was real, organized and high risk. If Lincoln was allowed to visit Baltimore, he would be leaving in a casket. Now, the detective just had to find and convince him.

Lincoln's journey had been a long one. He had been aboard the eponymously titled train since February 11 with a small detachment of colleagues, some press and his family. At every stop, he had spoken as loudly as he could muster for the enormous crowds and shaken innumerable hands, as every person had wanted to meet the "Rail Splitter." Yet, he knew the hardest part lay ahead. His inauguration wasn't until March 4. Then, the real challenges would begin.

On February 21, he and his entourage reached Philadelphia and attended yet another in a long line of dinners held in his honor at the Continental Hotel. Just the day before in the same city, Kate Warne, one of Pinkerton's operatives, had met with Norman Judd, one of Lincoln's entourage, and Colonel E.S. Sandford, president of the American Telegraph Company. She relayed Pinkerton's concerns, and they began working on informing—and convincing—Lincoln. Pinkerton, on the other hand, connected with Samuel Felton, who had initially hired him and shared the same evidence. Everyone agreed that Lincoln needed to be warned.

The group informed Lincoln of their concerns and suggested that he ride to Washington that very night. According to Pinkerton, Lincoln responded by saying, while he "fully appreciate[ed] these suggestions," he felt obligated to "raise the flag over Independence Hall to-morrow morning, and to visit the legislature at Harrisburg in the afternoon." He noted that the incoming president "had not evinced the slightest evidence of agitation or fear."[118]

The next day, Frederick Seward, William Seward's son, also spoke with Lincoln and passed along the same warnings as Pinkerton but on behalf of his

Allan Pinkerton, President Abraham Lincoln and Major General John A. McClernand at Antietam, Maryland, by Alexander Gardner, 1862. *Library of Congress.*

father and General Winfield Scott. With two different groups coming to the same conclusion, Lincoln became convinced. He would take a late train while dressed in disguise. The press would be holed up in a room, and telegraph lines would be cut to keep word from spreading. Only those who needed to know would be informed. It was a harebrained plan, but between Pinkerton's assurances and Seward's independent analysis, he must have felt that he had little choice. Honestly, the most difficult part most likely didn't involve any travel or secrecy at all. Lincoln had to tell his wife, Mary Todd, and he knew her reaction would be the equivalent of a volcano's eruption. Somehow, he managed to succeed in convincing her or in duping her about the truth.

The plan went off remarkably well. They reached Baltimore about 3:30 a.m. and continued through the city without being recognized. Eventually, Lincoln and Pinkerton made it to Washington, D.C., and safely to the Willard Hotel. They had outwitted any of their potential foes. Lincoln's family arrived later that day but exited the train safely before it was swamped at the depot.

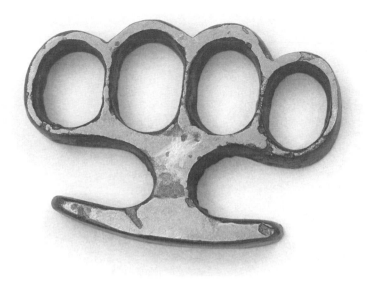

Brass knuckles carried by Abraham Lincoln's bodyguards during his train ride through Baltimore. Photography by Carol Highsmith, 2007. Artifact in the collection of Ford's Theatre, Washington, D.C. *Carol M. Highsmith's America, Library of Congress, Prints and Photographs Division.*

Goggles carried by Abraham Lincoln's bodyguards during his train ride through Baltimore. Photography by Carol Highsmith, 2007. Artifact in the collection of Ford's Theatre, Washington, D.C. *Carol M. Highsmith's America, Library of Congress, Prints and Photographs Division.*

Not surprisingly, the citizenry of Baltimore were upset at Lincoln's "midnight ride" and subsequent shunning of their city. Mayor George William Brown considered that the plot was created by the "frightened imaginations" of "some superserviceable persons," who only wanted to get "up a sensation of the first class."[119] The move had publicly humiliated the mayor, who had waited at the Calvert Street station to receive Lincoln. He reflected that if Lincoln had arrived and "spoken a few words…expressing the kind feelings which were in his heart with the simple eloquence of which he was so great a master," the city would have turned more in his favor. Instead, news of the possible conspiracy created "a hostile feeling against the city."[120]

Nor did all of Lincoln's own party believe that the threat was real. Lamon wrote about the plot in a biography of Lincoln. Like Brown, he considered the whole situation to be part of the political ambitions of Pinkerton, as well as the nature of his "peculiar profession." He didn't believe any conspiracy existed, writing, "It is perfectly manifest that there was no conspiracy—no conspiracy of a hundred, of fifty, of twenty, of three; no definite purpose in the heart of even one man to murder Mr. Lincoln at Baltimore."[121] He noted how Pinkerton's lists of suspects noticeably lacked "any person of eminence, power, or influence," even though Governor Thomas Hicks of Maryland had written a letter to a colleague asking for some "good men" to "kill Lincoln and his men." He felt that Pinkerton's case focused too much on small-time players, who were probably little more than big talkers.[122]

Would Lincoln have survived a visit to Baltimore? No one will ever know for certain either way. What is known is that bypassing the city only heightened the growing tension in an already divided state.

As incensed as the city was with its new president, the unhappiness grew tenfold with his response to the attack on Fort Sumter in South Carolina on April 12. Talk of secession had increased in recent months, and one by one, several states followed South Carolina's decision to leave the union. On April 17, Virginia seceded. Lincoln knew that if Maryland followed, the capital would be surrounded. He had to secure Washington, D.C., and maintain Maryland in the union. Faced with little choice, he ordered Northern troops to come to D.C., which meant that they would inevitably travel through Baltimore.

On the morning of Friday, April 19, several troops from the Sixth Regiment, Massachusetts Volunteer Militia, and the Washington Brigade

President Street Station. *Author photograph.*

of Philadelphia arrived at President Street Station on the Philadelphia, Wilmington & Baltimore line. Due to an old law, their cars were uncoupled and taken across Pratt Street by horse. Mayor George William Brown recounted in his memoir the route they planned, one that can be easily retraced today:

> *The train of thirty-five cars arrived at President-street Station at about eleven o'clock. The course which the troops had to take was first northerly on President street, four squares to Pratt street, a crowded thoroughfare leading along the heads of the docks, then along Pratt street west for nearly a mile to Howard street, and then south, on Howard street, one square to the Camden-street station.*[123]

A large crowd assembled to "give them an unwelcome reception." They began throwing paving stones at the cars, damaging windows. Several of the cars managed to continue to Camden Depot to connect with the Baltimore & Ohio Railroad. However, before the rest could pass, the crowd had managed to lay seven or eight anchors across the tracks. Even a large cart of sand was dumped onto the tracks to block the transport. The cars stopped, and as the soldiers waited, the mob began "lustily cheering for the South, for Jefferson Davis, South Carolina and secession, and groans for sundry obnoxious parties."[124]

Eventually, the troops organized and started marching. Only a percentage of the men were armed, and many were still in their civilian clothing. Captain A.S. Follansbee, commanding the troops, ordered a double-quick march, which gave the appearance that the soldiers were running. To the crowd, it looked like the troops were running from them, and they inferred that they weren't armed.

At some point, someone fired a shot. Chaos erupted.

Although Mayor Brown sympathized with the South, he still joined Captain Follansbee in heading the column of soldiers. Brown recounted how the troops responded, writing:

> *They* [the soldiers] *were firing wildly, sometimes backward, over their shoulders. So rapid was the march that they could not stop to take aim. The*

The Sixth Regiment of the Massachusetts Volunteers firing into the people in Pratt Street, while attempting to pass through Baltimore en route for Washington, April 19, 1861. Library of Congress.

mob, which was not very large, as it seemed to me, was pursuing with shouts and stones, and, I think, an occasional pistol-shot. The uproar was furious.[125]

Brown asked Follansbee to stop the quick march, and the soldiers slowed their pace. Instead of calming the people, the "mob grew bolder" and renewed its attack, even though its members were only armed with stones and a few pistols. The crowd rushed the soldiers, and some managed to pry muskets out of their hands. The soldiers fired at will, although there was no order given. The *Sun* continued the narrative, reporting at length on the violence as it grew:

People then ran in every direction in search of arms, but the armories of the military companies of the city were closely guarded and none could be obtained. The firing continued from Frederick street to South street in quick succession but how many fell cannot now be ascertained.[126]

Among those shot was a young boy on a ship in the Inner Harbor. The *Sun* reported that he was William Reed, "a hand on board the oyster sloop, *Wild Pigeon*," and that he "received a ball through the abdomen." He didn't survive the injury.[127]

Attack on the Massachusetts Sixth at Baltimore, April 19, 1861. *Library of Congress.*

Meanwhile, the troops that had succeeded in arriving at the Camden Depot fared only slightly better. Marshal George P. Kane headed about fifty police officers at the station. Throngs of people had been assembling there for hours. When the first cars arrived, the mob pressed against the windows, "presenting knives and revolvers, and cursed up into the faces of the soldiers." The police officers got in between to form a barrier as the men exited the cars. They boarded the train for Washington but were unable to move as the crowd surged around and tried obstructing the tracks. The police worked to remove the "great logs and telegraph poles," which required more than a dozen people to move.[128]

Marshal Kane and his officers headed back toward the fracas growing on Pratt Street. Again, they ran between the soldiers and the crowd, drawing their revolvers to keep as much of the mob at bay. The people began to back up, and the troops were able to continue to the trains without further assault. Eventually, the train was able to pass, and the crowd returned to the depot.

As the train passed a nearby lot, Robert W. Davis, a local dry goods merchant, began cheering for Jefferson Davis with some friends. One of the soldiers shot him from the window of the car. According to newspaper reports, he caught "nine musket balls in his left side."[129] Being well known, his death particularly riled the local community.

In all, at least twenty-one people were killed in the riot, including four members of the Sixth Massachusetts Volunteer Militia; six from the Twenty-sixth and Twenty-seventh Regiment Volunteer Infantry, "the Washington Brigade"; and eleven civilians from the city, including those mentioned before. Reports from the time were conflicting, and it is possible that more men died. Many more were wounded during the fight.

In response to the riot, James Ryder Randall, a Baltimorean living in Louisiana, wrote the poem "My Maryland," which eventually became the state song: "Maryland, My Maryland." Set to the tune of "Oh, Tannenbaum," the poem viciously attacks Lincoln and the Union. One stanza reads:

> *Dear Mother! burst the tyrant's chain,*
> *Maryland!*
> *Virginia should not call in vain,*
> *Maryland!*
> *She meets her sisters on the plain—*
> *"Sic semper!" 'tis the proud refrain*

That baffles minions back again,
Maryland!
Arise in majesty again,
Maryland! My Maryland![130]

The verse refers to Virginia's decision to secede and Randall's hope that Maryland would follow in its footsteps. The state never did. The state legislature met in the pro-Union town of Frederick, but it was never resolved. Before the special session could meet again in September, several members were arrested, and a vote was never taken. The song continues to serve as the state song today, although there have been several attempts to either remove it or change the lyrics.

While Baltimore served as home to the worst of the initial bloodshed of the war, it remained remarkably peaceful for the rest of it. This is largely due to the actions of General Benjamin Franklin Butler, who began occupying the city on May 13. In the immediate aftermath of the violence, Mayor Brown had purportedly organized burnings of several bridges north of the city to keep more troops from arriving. However, Butler arrived in Annapolis by steam ferry. He utilized his regiment of men from the Sixth and Eighth Massachusetts Volunteer Militia and Cook's Boston Artillery to first occupy Relay, a small community just outside Baltimore. Relay was important, as it stood where the Baltimore & Ohio Railroad was divided, with one section crossing the Patapsco River and the other heading west toward Harper's Ferry. Once Butler had control of the railroads, he was able to stop supplies from heading toward Confederate states.

On the evening of May 13, Butler brought his men, made up primarily of the riot veterans, into Baltimore and took control of Federal Hill. They trained their cannons on the city, flew the American flag and confiscated arms from local warehouses. Butler then sent a proclamation to the city, informing the citizens that rebelling would not be tolerated—including flying the Confederate flag. He declared martial law and arrested several prominent figures, including Mayor Brown and Marshal Kane. When Butler's superiors learned of his unauthorized actions, they were outraged and transferred him to Fortress Monroe in Virginia.

Still, a military presence remained in Baltimore. Fort McHenry became a prison for anyone suspected of being disloyal. The city remained divided politically for the remainder of the war.

Arrest of Marshal Kane, July 1861. *Library of Congress.*

Booth family plot in Greenmount Cemetery, featuring the unmarked grave of John Wilkes Booth. *Author photograph.*

Lincoln returned to Baltimore twice. In 1864, he was a speaker at a Sanitary Fair, which served to raise money to help care for wounded Union soldiers. Then, in 1865, his funeral train stopped in the city. Unlike his midnight ride, this special train received full honor from the city, which paid silent, weeping respect to the fallen president.

In a sad twist of irony, Baltimore serves as the final resting place for the man who did successfully assassinate Lincoln. In Greenmount Cemetery is the unmarked grave of John Wilkes Booth, whose family owned a plot there. While no one will ever know for certain what would have happened if Lincoln had stopped here in 1861, it seems that the city was fated to play a role in his death.

"Revolt on the Railroads"

The Great Strike of 1877

There had been a lawless outbreak Friday night, the tracks of [Camden Station] *were red with the blood of the slain.*
—*The* Sun, *July 27, 1877*

When your company is doing poorly, who do you continue to pay: your workers or your stockholders? This was the question placed before many railroad companies in 1877, including the Baltimore & Ohio Railroad (B&O). In the aftermath of the Civil War, railroad companies built throughout the country at an unprecedented pace, creating an unsustainable pattern of growth. Following the Panic of 1873, the bottom began to give way underneath the companies. Over the following years, many began cutting staff and the remaining employees' pay. While the B&O was one of the last to follow suit, it eventually felt forced into the same line of action. On July 11, 1877, B&O president John W. Garrett issued an order to his officers and employees, explaining that the board of directors had decided to reduce their pay by 10 percent due to "the depression in the general business interests of the country." He concluded the announcement with the hope that "every officer and man in the service will cheerfully recognize the necessity of the reduction." His hopes were immediately dashed.[131]

While the pay reduction was certainly a more humane choice than wholesale layoffs, it didn't help that workers' annual salaries were only around $400 a year, which was about $200 less than salaries at many other railroads. Worse, while the company would cover the cost to send a worker out as part of the train crew, it was out of the worker's pocket to pay for his return home.[132] In hindsight, it should not seem surprising that in a time before labor unions existed, the workers turned to the one weapon at their disposal: they went on strike.

On July 16, railroad workers in multiple states began their strike. The B&O brought in previously laid-off workers to help maintain operations. In Martinsburg, West Virginia, the strike had a more serious effect. At one of B&O's chief relay stations, about twenty-five strikers intimidated their replacements and extinguished the trains' fires, which completely halted all transportation in and out of the area. The strikers physically removed other workers from the trains. They were joined by a large crowd of local citizens, and the city had to call in reinforcements to try to preserve order.[133] By July 19, only two trains actually managed to leave from Martinsburg: one successfully entered Baltimore, and the other, heading west, was stopped by more strikers.[134]

At first, Baltimore remained fairly calm, but the mood darkened quickly. The strike soon reached Cumberland, Maryland, and unease spread like a virus across the railroads. On July 20, Governor John Lee Carroll sent out an order calling for military support to uphold the peace. In Baltimore, the bells rang 1-5-1, also known as the military call, which alerted the local regiments. However, they rang just as the citizenry was leaving work for the day, which resulted in bringing out the populace, who began congregating outside the various city armories. Nonetheless, 250 members of the Fifth Regiment of the Maryland National Guard assembled in the northwest section of the city (now the location of Maryland General Hospital) and began their march toward Camden Station. They were initially met by a "good-humored" crowd, who gave "demonstrations of applause." As they neared their destination, the atmosphere changed, and the applause gave way to "hoots and jeers."[135]

Things were worse for the Sixth Regiment at the armory on the corner of Fayette and Front Streets (where the central branch of Baltimore's Post Office sits today). Although the group was initially ordered to remain on duty at the armory, their instructions changed after the Fifth began encountering difficulties, and they were told to move out to Camden Station. Before they could even leave, a riot began outside the building. The *Baltimore American and Commercial Advertiser* suggested that the rioters were not employees of the B&O but rather "composed of in large part rowdies, loafers, and half-grown boys, who were never engaged in running railroad trains or any other honest employment."[136] It remains unknown whether the upstarts were employees, sympathizers or those simply looking for a fight. Either way, this unruly mix of people began smashing the building's windows and tossing pavement inside. The soldiers were forced to shoot their way out of the armory.[137]

Once outside, the Sixth Regiment marched toward Camden Station. The *Sun* reported what they encountered outside:

> *The scene from Front Street up to the depot, Camden st., [sic] was one of terror. The firing continued at quick intervals from the armory's long distance up Baltimore street. Several times, it was as though platoons were firing…The streets were quickly deserted and the detachment passed on by* The Sun *office.*[138]

The Great Strike, 1877. Library of Congress.

At least nine men were killed, and more were injured during the ensuing battle. Only fifty-nine members of the Sixth Regiment eventually arrived at the depot after enduring several more blocks of fighting.

Once inside, the soldiers entered the waiting cars, only to discover that the rioters had torn up the tracks themselves. "The demonstration against the engineer and fireman was so great that they were compelled to desert the engine, having first been stoned by the mob," reported the *Sun*. "The engine was afterwards completely disabled by stones thrown at it by the mob."[139] An estimated fifteen thousand people surrounded the area. By 10:00 p.m., they started a fire on the south end of the passenger platform, in some of the depot's sheds and in three of the passenger cars. The fire department tried putting out the flames, only to be stopped by the densely packed crowd.

Even with the soldiers and about two hundred police officers, Governor Carroll knew that the city was ill equipped to handle the riot. He immediately telegraphed President Rutherford B. Hayes for assistance. Troops from Fort McHenry and surrounding states headed toward Baltimore to help dispel the violence.

During the middle of the night, the mob finally started to disperse, and the fire was put out. The remaining soldiers and police officers continued to guard the depot against any additional threat, and Governor Carroll issued another telegraph to the president, informing him of the tentative quiet. The secretary of war, George W. McCrary, responded with the promise to send five hundred marines to "promptly quell any further disturbance."

On Saturday, the governor distributed an order advising people to stay in their homes and "abstain from gathering in crowds." People obliged during the day, but at night, a group tried burning one of the B&O's barges in Fells Point. They succeeded in burning both a building on the west side of the city and a train just beyond the city limits.[140] Later that evening, another crowd gathered at Eutaw and Camden Streets. The police advanced on the mob. They arrested several members, who were taken to the depot to be watched by the Fifth Regiment. The *Baltimore American and Commercial Advertiser* estimated that over two hundred were "in jail to be dealt with according to the law."[141] Only a portion went to trial, as the authorities were aware that they would be unable to persecute the ringleaders.

By Sunday, nearly two thousand Federal troops arrived in the city. Given the large force, there were no more demonstrations in Baltimore, and workers returned to the railways to clean up and rebuild. The state estimated that the riots cost more than $85,000 to suppress, but this number did include the cost the riots inflicted on the local economy, as many businesses suffered with the breakdown of transportation.[142] At the same time as the riots, workers from the Chesapeake & Ohio Canal had also been striking and "had tied up their boats to the banks of the canal, and had assumed so threatening an attitude against any one who might wish to use that highway by trade that the route became entirely suspended."[143] Given the economic depression that had precipitated both events, it is unknown how far-reaching the cost and effect of the strikes ultimately were in Maryland.

While peace was maintained in Baltimore, rioting spread to other cities—from Pittsburgh to Albany to Chicago to Louisville and beyond. Many cities experienced even larger losses of life and property than what had happened in Baltimore. The riots lasted into August before they were finally and completely quelled.

The strikes did bring about changes at the B&O. In 1880, the company started the Baltimore and Ohio Employees' Association, which was designed to pay employees if they became sick or hurt by a job-related accident. They soon added a pension plan and death benefits, as well.[144] Historians today credit the strikes with helping to birth the labor union movement of the early twentieth century. While large and unruly, they laid the seeds for a more comprehensive and organized structure to help benefit workers' rights.

Did She or Didn't She?

The Case of the "Baltimore Borgia"

W as Ellen (also known as Elizabeth) Wharton a murderer? The society woman, who was considered "of engaging manner," left an apparent laundry list of victims in her path. She became known as the "Baltimore Borgia," after Lucrezia Borgia, a sixteenth-century Italian woman who was rumored to poison people by hiding the fatal compounds within her ring's secret compartment.

A widow, Wharton (née Nugent) came from a prominent Philadelphia family and had been married to Major Henry Wharton. She had many admirers and was considered to be particularly affectionate and devoted to her family, which included two adult children: a son and a daughter. When her husband died mysteriously in the late 1860s, no one felt anything but sorrow for Wharton's loss. Again, they felt sympathy for her when her son died soon after—most likely unaware that she had taken out a $30,000 life insurance policy on him. Soon, there were more condolences to be made after her brother-in-law, Edward Wharton, died at her house during a visit, with his daughter—her niece—following soon after. However, it would take two more deaths in 1871 to make everyone look back and wonder: had she killed them all, or was she simply the victim of perennial bad luck?[145]

In late June 1871, Eugene Van Ness became sick during a visit to Wharton's house on Hamilton Terrace at Eutaw Street. He had been "given a glass of beer or punch, and soon after drinking it was attacked with illness, and fell upon the floor of the dining room." Van Ness, a bookkeeper for Alexander

Brown & Sons, became so ill that he was forced to remain at the house for several days.[146] Fortunately, he recovered.

However, when General William Scott Ketchum stayed at Wharton's home, starting on June 28, the situation worsened. Ketchum had been good friends with Henry Wharton. Within a few days of his stay, he suddenly fell ill and died. An autopsy revealed about twenty grams of tartar emetic (also known as antimony potassium tartrate) in his system. In that amount, tartar emetic—a poison—is lethal.[147] Ketchum, a widower, left behind two children.[148] Dr. S.C. Chew, one of the doctors on the case, went back and had Van Ness's glass examined as well. It was found to contain fifteen grams of tartar emetic.[149]

On July 10, Wharton was arrested for poisoning both men.[150] Since she was apparently "suffering from liver complaint" and possible seizures, she was not immediately taken to jail but was placed under house arrest. The police questioned her daughter, Nellie, and two of the family's servants.[151] After formally indicting Wharton, they took her to the jail. Nellie voluntarily stayed with her in the cell. The case drew immediate attention from across the city, and Wharton's condition while in jail was reported regularly in the newspapers.

Where did the tartar emetic come from? Wharton freely admitted to purchasing sixty grams of it from Gosman & Co. and "used it in a mustard plaster which she placed upon her breast."[152] The compound had regularly been utilized for medicinal purposes, notably as a vomit inducer, an expectorant and to produce sweating. However, it was also a dangerous ingredient, even in small amounts. Soon, officials would add "tincture of yellow jasmine" to the list of poisons used in the fatal drinks. While used in moderation as a muscle relaxer, it is possible to overdose on the ingredient.[153]

Why would she attempt to murder either of the men? According to friends of Ketchum's, he had come to Baltimore to collect on a $2,500 promissory note made to Wharton, but the police couldn't find evidence of the note's existence. Kethchum's brother-in-law, General Benjamin W. Brice, testified that Wharton had visited him only a few days after Ketchum's death, asking for "$4,000 worth of government bonds which she had deposited for safe-keeping with Gen. Ketchum." She claimed to have paid back the original promissory note and had ripped up the original note "in his presence."[154]

Additionally, her sister-in-law, Mrs. J.G. Wharton, wrote to the *Washington Star* (republished in the *Sun*) her belief that Wharton had poisoned her husband Edward, their daughter and herself during their trip nearly four years earlier.

Only she survived. She claimed that Wharton owed her late husband $2,500, which she only received "with difficulty…after his death." In the letter, she explained that she had tried implicating Wharton earlier. but her doctors had thought that her "mind was affected" and silenced her suspicions.[155]

Meanwhile, the *New York Times* diagnosed Wharton—from afar—as having a neurotic disorder. Besides the murders at hand, they looked back at a strange incident from earlier in her life, which had been previously reported on by the *Sun*. When Wharton was a young woman, she had lived a privileged life. All of her wishes were indulged, people lavished attention upon her and she had many male admirers. So, her friends and family were not surprised when they received an invitation to her upcoming wedding, which was to occur in her family's mansion. Dressed like a queen, she awaited her groom, Mr. Williamson, while surrounded by a crowd of attendees. He never showed. Messengers went to find him, and when they returned, they had a perplexing response: "Mr. Williamson had not contracted the marriage and knew nothing about it."[156]

Concerned about his daughter's mental health, her father decided to send her away to an asylum. However, she ran off and eloped with Lieutenant Henry Wharton. She was considered "passionately devoted" to her husband.[157]

The case was removed to Annapolis in December, given its high-profile nature. Even so, the courthouse was regularly filled to the brim with spectators, primarily from Baltimore.[158] Over 160 witnesses were called during the extended trial, which lasted for forty-three days. Chemical experts from across the country were put on the stand. The cost for the trial reached over $10,000.[159]

The chemists' testimonies were often inconsistent and even contradictory. They pointed out that "traces of arsenic and antimony can be found in every human body" and called into question the examination of Ketchum's corpse.[160] Additional questions were raised about his symptoms and the nature of his death. They debated whether tartar emetic was the actual cause or whether he had suffered from meningitis or some other issue.

Given the uncertainty, it is not surprising that Wharton was acquitted of the murder. The *New York Tribune* agreed with the finding, believing that the entire case was circumstantial: "Nobody saw Mrs. Wharton administer poison to General Ketchum, and when the learned experts came into court to apply 'unerring rules' of science to the case, lay minds were at once confused and baffled." The *New York Sun* felt that "this case will accomplish a great good by

Trial of Mrs. Wharton, sketch by James E. Taylor, 1871. *Library of Congress.*

rendering it scarcely possible to convict a person of murder by poisoning without the clearest proof of presence of a sufficient quantity of poison to produce death…But how many persons have been hanged without such proof?"[161]

The second trial regarding the attempted poisoning of Eugene Van Ness occurred in the beginning of 1878. It produced a hung jury. Wharton was never taken to trial for any of the other deaths, even though an attempt was made to autopsy her son's body. The results were inconclusive. After the trials ended, the *Sun* updated the public on her life in 1879:

> [Wharton] *removed to a small Pennsylvania town, and has ever since sought a quiet and secluded life. She is accompanied here by a daughter, with whom she is always seen…but always smiling, always cheerful, always motherly, and yet the trouble through which she has passed would have placed many another woman beneath the sod long ago.*[162]

Her daughter eventually married William Moore Wharton, and they all lived together outside Philadelphia. Ellen Wharton died in 1890, around the age of seventy.[163]

Burking, Bodies and Baltimore

G enerally, the University of Maryland is a testament to educational achievement in Maryland, but it also has a darker past connected to grave robbing and murder. Davidge Hall, the university's medical branch, is housed in downtown Baltimore, not far from Westminster Hall—the final resting place of Edgar Allan Poe. Today, the school is a world-class training facility. However, in the nineteenth century, the university was not just known for its medical acumen but also for the price it paid for fresh, dead bodies. The corpses were dissected and used as educational tools. They were collected by Frank "the Body-Snatcher," who would follow funerals to Westminster Hall and then lie in wait to dig up the graves on behalf of the school. (Read more in Christopher Scharpf's foreword.)

The act of killing a person by suffocation, which would leave the body more intact for potential sale to physicians, is known as "burking." The term dates back to about 1829, when Scotsman William Burke was convicted and hanged for a series of murders with the intent of selling the corpses. His accomplice, William Hare, escaped hanging by testifying against Burke.[164] According to their testimony, they killed about thirty people, although Burke refused to give the exact number. When asked how "these fearful atrocities [were] perpetrated," Burke responded that they used suffocation, explaining:

We made the persons drunk, and then suffocated them by holding the nostrils and mouth, and getting on the body. Sometimes I held the mouth and nose, while Hare went upon the body; and sometimes Hare held the mouth and nose, while I placed myself on the body. Hare has perjured himself by what he said at the trial about the murder of Docherty. He did not sit by while I did it, as he says. He was on the body assisting me with all his might, while I held the nostrils and mouth with one hand, choked her under the throat with the other. We sometimes used a pillow, but did not in this case.[165]

Even after these infamous crimes, the University of Maryland continued to pay for bodies to use in its school. There were few laws governing the practice at the time.

In 1886, assistant janitor Anderson Perry claimed that a stranger offered him a body for the University of Maryland to use. According to Perry, he accepted the offer and promised to pay the man fifteen dollars the following morning. After receiving the body, he noticed "marks of violence" upon it and went to Dr. Herbert Harlan with his suspicions. Dr. Harlan examined the body and "found that the temples and head had been crushed and that there were two deep puncture marks in the left breast."[166] Confirming Perry's concerns, he contacted the police, who started investigating.

The coroner and another doctor conducted an autopsy together, which led them to believe that the injuries had occurred postmortem. The police were not convinced. Marshal Frey and other detectives began calling other stations to check missing persons reports. By Sunday, they learned that a woman was missing from Pig Alley, located between Paca and Eutaw Streets—and not far from the school. They brought in eleven-year-old Sarah Blockson, who identified the body as sixty-year-old Emily Brown, one of her mother, Mary Blockson's, tenants. Blockson corroborated her daughter's identification.

Emily Brown had already suffered through a difficult life. Originally from Easton, Maryland, she started out as a dressmaker before becoming addicted to morphine and opium.[167] After moving to Baltimore, she regularly begged for alms to pay the weekly $2.50 she owed Blockson for rent. Most weeks, she only managed around fifty cents, and sometimes, she couldn't give anything. Blockson claimed that Brown "spent most of the money she got by begging on whiskey and was frequently intoxicated."[168]

On the Friday that Emily Brown was killed, Mary Blockson had ordered her to "go out and beg or leave the house for good." She went off but apparently returned while Blockson was out. At some point during that time, Brown was murdered.

The police found Perry's story suspicious. They arrested him, and he subsequently pointed them toward two other men, John Thomas Ross and Albert Hawkins. Ross was Blockson's son by her first husband. She was set to marry Perry the following week. The police detained her as a witness to the crime.

During his interrogation, Ross confessed to murdering Emily Brown. He said that Perry had offered him a way to make some money by killing Brown and selling her body to the university. Ross said that he then brought Hawkins in to stand watch as he went into the house "holding a brick hid in my hand. I said not a word to alarm the old woman, and while she was suspecting nothing, I suddenly struck a blow on her head, crushing in her skull. I then went out and took Hawkins's place while he went in and stabbed her to make sure of it."[169]

The case was sensational in its time, and although the assailants didn't suffocate Brown, it was still referred to as "burking" because of the planned disposal of the body afterward to the medical school. Perry was acquitted for his role in the crime, and charges against Hawkins were initially dropped due to a lack of evidence.[170] He was later convicted and sentenced.[171] Ross was convicted in a brief, one-day trial but attempted to argue against the use of his confession to the court of appeals.[172] The court, however, found that the confession was admissible, and Ross was hanged for the crime.[173]

Although Perry escaped the penitentiary and the noose, he died not long after being set free. In a strange twist, his body was given to the university for "students' use." However, the part of the building where his body was being held caught fire, consuming his remains.[174]

In 1890, the State Board of Anatomy issued the "Anatomy Act," which provided strict guidelines on how the university could receive corpses. Other Maryland schools continued to use bodies for educational purposes. Any not immediately used were stored at Johns Hopkins University.[175]

Playing "Winder"

The Escape and Capture of Ike Winder

In the early twentieth century, young children played on the streets well into the evening. Some of their games would be familiar today: tag, I spy, hare and hounds and more. However, one game called "Winder" might not ring a bell with modern kids—perhaps because it was based on a sensational trial that captivated the city in 1906.

In December of the previous year, two men—Isaac "Ike" and his nephew William Charles Winder—drank heartily at the Eight-Mile House on York Road in Towson, just north of the city. Apparently, they frightened the owner's wife and ran off clutching bottles of whiskey and gin. Afterward, they reportedly broke into the home of Frederick T. Rinehart, a sixty-five-year-old tollgate keeper on Dulaney Valley Pike. His small, two-story frame house sat at the foot of a hill, not far from a bridge over a run. Rinehart had fallen asleep on his lounge when the Winders smashed in a window and the upper part of the door. Beside him lay a small pistol, little more than a toy. He tried using it.

The details of what happened next are uncertain, although it's thought that robbery was the motive. At least three shots were fired. One hit Charles Winder. Another hit a wall. The final one landed in Rinehart's back.

Rinehart's wife came downstairs and into the room, but the men had already disappeared. The club used to break the window and door lay on the floor, not far from a bottle of gin. Rinehart's chair was "smashed to splinters." She found her husband lying askew. In a newspaper report, she recounted her response:

"My God!" I said, "what's the matter?" But he did not answer me. Then his arms twitched and he gasped once. I thought he was stunned and ran back into the kitchen after some spirits of camphor. As I was pouring some on his head I noticed the bullet hole in his jacket and then I saw his eyes—so glassy-like.[176]

Unfortunately, he was already dead. Scared for her life and the lives of the couple's children, she ran back upstairs and kept watch, hoping the men would not return. Eventually, someone came, wanting the tollgate opened.

Mrs. Rinehart recognized the driver as Mary Cook and told her that her husband had been murdered. Cook immediately took off for Rinehart's closest neighbor and brought John Schmidt back with her. News spread through the area, and soon police officers came to the scene. Dr. R.C. Massenburg, chief of police, performed an autopsy on Rinehart. He determined that the bullet had killed Rinehart in less than a minute.

During the ensuing investigation, the detectives found a trail of blood starting in front of the victim's house. The drops continued "across the bridge and to the top of the hill" before culminating at the side of the road. Nearby were footprints and another bottle with just a tiny bit of gin left inside. With these clues and the testimony from Mrs. James W. Shea of the Eight-Mile House, they had gathered enough evidence to start seeking out suspects.

Soon, they determined that one of the men was Charles Winder, an African American man who was being treated for a bullet wound in the abdomen at Maryland General Hospital. According to the staff, Winder claimed that he had accidentally shot himself. As the wound was minor, the hospital treated and released him—but not before taking his name and address. The authorities quickly caught up with the Winders.

A trial quickly followed, and the men were found guilty. The younger Winder was given eighteen years, but Ike was sentenced to hang on March 30, 1906. However, on March 5, he escaped from the Towson jail. According to Winder, he took advantage of a commotion "the crazy man upstairs" made over water:

He wanted water, and he wouldn't take it from the night watchman but wanted the warden to bring it to him. Then the warden went up there, and the man kept on hollering and jumping up and down over my head, and so the warden called for help. Then the night man ran up there. In a minute he came down and I asked him what was the matter with the lunatic. So the watchman stopped to show me what the crazy man was doing. The crazy man, he said, was pulling at his cell door, as if he wanted to get the iron doors open. The watchman showed me just how the crazy one was doing. Then, when the night man had gone back upstairs, I thought to myself, "This ought to be a good chance for me to go." So I lifted on the door and it came open.[177]

When examining the cell, others said that he climbed up and lifted the bar. At the gallows, Winder relented that he had indeed broken out of the cell by breaking off the handle of his water bucket and fashioning a device to unbolt the door.[178] After escaping his cell, Winder jumped out of an unlocked window.

He spent fifteen days free—most of them in Baltimore. After running away, he found family and friends, including a man who owed him money. At one point, he was found by Sheriff Elliott, who shot at him. Winder ran and escaped again, finding refuge at an empty farmhouse. Eventually, he jumped on a streetcar on Harford Avenue but suspected that he had been recognized when "the motorman and conductor got off and entered a saloon." He fled the scene and found another streetcar on Gay Street. From there, he went down to Belair Market and "Pat" Fry's saloon. He stayed in the city until that Saturday evening, heading to Highlandtown and then walking across to Gardenville.

On March 20, Baltimore County police marshal Abraham J. Street found Winder as he "was making a small fire in the woods." He wasn't armed and didn't resist. He was taken back to jail, and his execution remained scheduled for March 30. The *Sun* remarked that even though he was a convicted murderer, "in many quarters sympathy was expressed for Winder…because of the remarkable fight he made for freedom."[179]

To pay for his funeral, Winder's spiritual advisor, Reverend J.L. Amos, applied for a permit to exhibit Winder's body in his church after his hanging. He planned to charge ten cents a person. The authorities initially refused to issue the permit, believing that it would incite a "great gathering of hysterical colored people who will create a disturbance in the neighborhood and give the police much trouble."[180] Hypocritically, the authorities offered tickets to five hundred people for the hanging itself. More than two thousand arrived to witness the event.

In the late morning, Winder was led to the gallows. As the noose lowered around his neck, he tried fighting off the men surrounding him—all five of them. He failed. They hanged him, only to discover that he had tried desperately to survive, having managed to fit two fingers beneath the rope just before he fell. However, his neck was broken, and he died almost instantly.

The case raised concerns not only about the murder itself and security at the jail but also about racial inequality in Maryland. Booker T. Washington went on to mention the Winder case in his book *The Story of the Negro: The Rise of the Race from Slavery*, volume two, noting how his trial and execution

> *cost the state $2,000 more than it cost to educate one of the graduates of the Coloured High School. Assuming that Ike Winder, if he had been graduated from the high school, would have done as well as the other graduates, the state lost, not only the money expended in convicting and executing him, but it lost the economic value of an educated citizen.*[181]

And the child's game? Apparently it involved someone playing "the killer," who would write cryptic notes on paper scraps and leave them along a trail. Soon, a "posse" would pursue the killer by following the notes left behind. The point of the game was to leave a convoluted and difficult course. However, the game and its historical connections soon gave way to other pastimes, and the story of Winder, the murder and his escape all drifted away as well.

The Sordid Findings of Baltimore's Vice Commission

Tucked away in the closed stacks of the Enoch Pratt Free Library's main branch is a rarely seen report. The report was considered to be so incendiary that the general public refused to acknowledge its existence, ashamed of how it aired their collective dirty laundry. On its onion-thin pages, this five-volume report comprehensively detailed the lives of Baltimore's "working girls." Conducted by a vice commission, reports like these were typical to many of the big cities during the Progressive era, a time of great social reform across the country at the turn of the twentieth century.

In 1913, Governor Phillips Lee Goldsborough appointed the commission, which included two women. The commission members acted as investigators, spending countless hours staking out suspected brothels, interviewing workers and pretending to apply for rooms in seedy houses. They medically examined workers, critiqued their living environments and reviewed trends in the field. While their methods were sometimes questionable, their findings illuminated an oft-buried history, providing a complex picture of the life of a prostitute.

The investigators were thorough in their report, and while they attempted to be objective by including hundreds of case studies, their inherent bias against prostitution is evident. They viewed the workers as pitiful and hopeless. After examining nearly 300 women, some of their worst suspicions were confirmed:

> [The women] *do not know that they have, or will shortly have, gonorrhea or syphilis; they do not see that they are becoming more and more unfit every day for any other kind of life and they do not understand that in a few, a very few, years, they will either be dead or turned adrift to a dreary hopeless poverty.*[182]

In 289 blood samples taken from the workers, they found that 63 percent tested positive for syphilis.[183] An additional 92 percent of 266 women examined were found to have gonorrhea.[184]

At the same time, they couldn't help but note that "many of these girls, in fact most of them, seem satisfied and believe that their lives as prostitutes are more desirable than what they had before."[185] By becoming prostitutes, numerous women had escaped difficult lives, often involving tumultuous relationships or having to toil away in factories or as domestics. Several had previously been "kept" by a man until the relationship ended, had been mistreated by family members or had been promiscuous with friends and strangers before entering the profession full time. According to investigators, some initially started out as street walkers or "charity girls," which they defined as teenagers who made themselves available to men at "dance halls, moving pictures, or shore parks" before turning to the relative security of a brothel.[186]

As prostitutes, the women now enjoyed very few responsibilities. The investigators noted that they "get up when they feel like it; they loll lazily about all day."[187] In describing an average day, the report says:

> *The customary routine in the better class houses would be for the girls to get up about eleven o'clock; dress themselves in kimonas* [sic] *and have breakfast. During the afternoon they would receive any men who may come. Dinner would be served about six. They would then dress and be ready for their customers about eight. The real "trading period," as they call it, extends from eight o'clock in the evening until four in the morning; it is at its heights from ten to twelve...The girls have one free afternoon and evening once a week, when they can go wherever they wish; if they stay longer than this, or go out at other times, they are fines from $5.00 to $10.00.*[188]

The report specified how a patron would engage with the women. The investigators spent several nights observing the brothels and sometimes even entering them. In great detail, they described how a man would be enticed to go in and the pleasantries that followed:

> *The madam herself meets him at the door with such greetings as: "Come right along in, I have some nice girls for you"... Two or three girls promptly come in, sit down and chat. They soon ask the stranger for money to start the piano, and before the strict regulations in regard to alcohol were in effect, a new comer was always requested to buy drinks. These are the conventional preliminaries. After they are over, the man selects a girl and they go upstairs together.* [189]

While the report recognized that the women often made tidy sums— ranging from around twenty to seventy-five dollars a week—few of them managed to save their earnings, and even fewer had much to show after several years of service.[190] Much of their earnings went to the madam, as well as to the items she "provided" at a higher price than in many of the local stores. The report details the various arrangements many of the madams had with suppliers to include an extra 10 percent or more to the cost of the goods. Others peddled it away on alcohol and drugs. Interestingly, many had entered the profession specifically because of the money.[191] Patrons spent anywhere from twenty-five cents to twenty-five dollars on a visit, depending on where the house was located, the race of the workers and how long he desired to stay.[192]

According to the commission investigators, only a small number of the women ever left the lifestyle permanently. While some became madams and some married for better or for worse, many ended up returning to the profession after attempting to work in another field. Of those who remained, most eventually succumbed to a sexually transmitted disease, drug or alcohol addiction, tuberculosis or suicide. The commissioners encountered only a few who survived past the age of sixty.[193]

When published, the report was met with outrage. Acclaimed Baltimore writer Henry Louis "H.L." Mencken despised such "Puritanical" commissions in general, claiming that "the 'investigation' of the social evil becomes an orgy, and that the ensuing 'report' of the inevitable 'vice commission' is made up of two parts sensational fiction and three parts platitude."[194] Mayor James H. Preston called it "a scandalous libel on life in Baltimore" and claimed that "no such conditions" existed in the city.[195] Other city council members joined the mayor in denouncing the report. However, the idea that they didn't know prostitution occurred in Baltimore was ludicrous. For years, the city had instituted an annual "Ladies' Day," during which madams paid a court-ordered fine of five to seventy-five dollars for running brothels in the city.[196] Ladies' Day provided a convenient method for the city to ignore the illicit profession while gaining revenue from it.

Still, the report led to significant changes in the city. In 1915, the Board of Police Commissioners decreed that "all assignation houses in the city be closed within ten days from that date [April 12] and at the same time provided for the gradual elimination after sixty days notice in each case of all houses of prostitution" with the intent that the brothels would be "wiped out" by September.[197] While prostitution inevitably continued, it no longer received any sort of backhanded approval from the city's administration.

Billie Holiday, by Carl Van Vechten, 1949. *Carl Van Vechten Photograph Collection, Library of Congress.*

Coincidentally, 1915 was also the year that Eleanora Fagan was born, although she's better known today by her stage name of Billie Holiday. There is dispute about whether Holiday was born in Baltimore or in Philadelphia. Either way, she inherited the post–vice commission style of brothels. When she was only twelve years old, she was introduced to Ethel Moore's "good-time house" at 20 Bond Street in Fells Point. A good time house was "an all-night party place where black Baltimoreans came not to buy sex specifically, but to dance, drink, smoke a reefer, and perhaps rent a room for an hour or two."[198] From Moore's, Fagan moved on to Alice Dean's bordello, where she was remembered as being a favorite with the men and the "youngest of all of the girls…All the women were jealous of her because she was light-complected, well-built, and she could sing." In her autobiography, Holiday claims that she only ran errands at Alice Dean's and that, more importantly, it was where she was introduced to Louis Armstrong and Bessie Smith on the bar's expensive Victrola.[199] While her childhood was difficult, she was able to transcend it with her wit and beautiful, languorous voice.

The Captain's Hotel. *Author photograph.*

Meanwhile, the report quietly disappeared into the library, nearly lost to history. Today, the city still faces difficulties with prostitution. Nonetheless, some residents have reclaimed parts of its history. Historians note how jazz icon Eubie Blake got his start playing at Aggie Shelton's bordello in 1898.[200] There's a local story floating around that the word "hooker" has its origins in the prostitutes who kicked around the hook-shaped Fells Point neighborhood. Whether or not this is true is debatable, but there is no doubt that the area was once home to several houses of ill repute. Nor does the neighborhood shy away from its more sordid past. The bar Red Star on Wolfe Street claims its name comes from the stars that women painted on their homes to advertise themselves to sailors. During a tour with the Fells Point GhostWalk, visitors hear about how prostitutes draped their petticoats from window to window to announce their intents. The Fells Point Preservation Society preserves the old Captain's Hotel on Aliceanna Street, which was a "quality" brothel dating back to the eighteenth century. Undoubtedly, Baltimore embraces its heritage—warts and all.

The Block

An old joke goes this way: "My father told me never to go to a burlesque show 'cause I'd see something I shouldn't see. Finally, I went to a burlesque show. He was right; I did see something I shouldn't see. I saw my father sitting in the second row."[201]

On December 6, 2010, a five-alarm fire broke out on Baltimore's infamous Block—that glittery, multicolored stretch of Baltimore Street that is home to several strip clubs, bars and tattoo parlors. While no one was hurt, the fire devastated several buildings, including the Gayety Show World Theater. Initial reports indicated that someone inside Yellow Booth No. 8, a peepshow stall inside the building, started the fire.[202] The blaze destroyed four buildings in total and forced the evacuation of twenty thousand area workers. Eyewitnesses saw showgirls running out into the bitter winter air, wearing little more than the jackets some of the patrons lent them.

There's a strange twist of irony in the Gayety Show World Theater burning, as it was originally the home of Lubin's Theater, one of the earliest entertainment venues on the Block, having been constructed about 1907. Perhaps even stranger is the fact that Lubin's and the idea of the Block were birthed from a fire—one that decimated most of the downtown.

In February 1904, the city's downtown was ravaged by the worst fire in its history. After starting on the morning of Sunday, February 7, at Hopkins Place and Liberty Street, the fire quickly grew, swiftly eating its way through the heart of Baltimore. In addition to the municipal fire department,

Fire damage on the Block. *Author photograph.*

assistance came from as far away as D.C., Philadelphia and New York. Unfortunately, the visiting firemen were unable to attach their hoses to the city's hydrants, stymieing their ability to assist. The *Sun*, whose own buildings were destroyed, still covered the scene of destruction, writing:

> *A high wind blowing from the time the fire began and continuing throughout Sunday and yesterday filled the air with myriads of cinders, which spread the conflagration to unexpected quarters. Dynamite was used frequently, but without satisfactory results. It seemed almost from the first that the firemen were doomed to make a losing fight despite their brave and vigorous efforts.*[203]

As the fire headed east, nothing was able to mitigate its appetite. Eventually, the firemen looked to the Jones Fall Canal, which bisected the downtown from Jonestown and Fells Point, as their last resort for controlling the situation. On Monday afternoon, thirty-seven steam fire engines from across the Mid-Atlantic created a "wall of water" using the falls to finally

The *Sun* building after the Baltimore fire, 1904. *Library of Congress.*

stop the fire's advance. Although the major fire was finished by mid-afternoon, it would take the city weeks to exterminate all the minor fires that smoldered throughout the charred remains of the downtown.[204] Overall, the fire destroyed about 140 acres, including 1,256 buildings.[205]

Before the fire destroyed the area, most of Baltimore Street was dedicated to retail and office space, with some manufacturing tucked away on the upper floors of buildings. Much of the area was already migrating to Howard Street due to rising rents, but the fire sped up the process of change. After the destruction, Philadelphia-based entrepreneur Sigemund Lubin decided to expand his enterprises in the city. He had already constructed a theater in 1902. In 1907, he created the first-known "double theater" at 404–06 East Baltimore Street. The downstairs was an inexpensive nickelodeon. Upstairs was the more expensive theater, featuring vaudeville acts and movies. He soon added the building next door to create an even larger triple-theater complex. It was immediately a popular place for people of all ages.[206]

Maurice Cohen, who later bought Lubin's and turned it into the Plaza, remembered the progression of theaters along the Block. "After Lubin's," he said, "came the Grand Theater, the Globe, the Clover, the Rivoli, Embassy,

Gayety, and undoubtedly, a few I've overlooked."[207] Interspersed with the theaters were lunchrooms, bars, clothing and other retail shops. The Block at the time actually spanned several blocks and was a major destination—not only for local residents but also for families as far away as Pennsylvania and D.C. Early entertainment included films, vaudeville and musical acts.

When did the Block change to focusing on adult entertainment? According to Cohen, his brother Max introduced a new twist at his bar, the Oasis, which he ran from 1927 to 1945. The hostesses were "seated around the place, dressed in evening gowns, chatting with the customers. Then the music would strike up, and the hostesses would peel off their gowns to reveal scanty costumes underneath, and go into various dance routines."[208] He didn't require his hostesses to be particularly talented or even necessarily beautiful. Trying to capitalize on the "anything-goes atmosphere" of the Oasis, he advertised the club as "the worst show and the best time in the world."[209] Some credit Cohen with introducing striptease to the city. Others say that he only had the women strip due to a lack of dressing area space.

Even as racier burlesque became more popular on the Block, visitors could also find major theater stars and comedians in the various arenas. John and Ethel Barrymore were spotted inside some of the clubs. John Barrymore famously recited Hamlet's soliloquy at the Oasis one night during a visit. John Nickel, whose father, John "Hon" Nickel, ran the venerable Gayety Theatre (different from the Gayety Show Theater), talked about the variety of performers there, recalling:

> For 60 years the Gayety brought to Baltimore this country's finest burlesque talents—strippers like Ann Corio, Margie Hart, Hinda Wassau, Blaze Starr, Valerie Parks, the Carroll Sisters, and such funny men as Phil Silvers, Jackie Gleason, Joe Penner, Rags Ragland, Red Skelton, Billy Hagen, Hap Hyatt, Billy Bob Reed.[210]

He went on to remark about the diversity of the audience—from married couples to senators and generals—who came to see the performers. Another former employee of the Gayety and a boxer in the 1930s, Joe Finazzo, recalled some of the other features of the theater:

> Beer at The Gayety cost 50 cents a bottle even through the '50s. On Friday nights they had a burlesque and boxing show that ran from 9 p.m. until 2 a.m.

Gayety Theatre. *Historic American Buildings Survey, Library of Congress.*

and was only a dollar. It was even cheaper if you wanted to sit in the peanut gallery. You got there by going up the fire escape from the alley to the third-floor upper balcony. No one really asked for age cards—if you looked 18, they let you in. If you didn't look old enough, back down the fire escape you went.[211]

The Gayety stands today, operating as Larry Flynt's Hustler Club. Its historic ornate façade remains well maintained, although the old marquee with its signature kicking girl is long gone, replaced by a large Hustler's sign.

As movies became increasingly popular, the theaters on the Block focused on more risqué shows. In 1932, the Hayes Code started, which restricted films' content, especially regarding sex and innuendo. Nudity was banned on the big screen. For the theater operators in Baltimore, this presented an opportunity to offer something that the movies couldn't: live women in suggestive costumes and poses. Interestingly, people today might have found many of the acts to be fairly modest by modern standards.[212]

Some of the famous routines on the Block included Moana's gold dance, in which she coated her entire body in gold paint. If she left the paint on for more than an hour, she could faint, and if it was left on even longer, the paint was potentially fatal. Other routines included Peggy Clarke, who danced with snakes, lizards and even a crocodile. Sally Rand had her fan dance, which left

Gayety Theatre. *Author photograph.*

little to the imagination. And there was Blaze Starr's fire routine, in which she lay across a loveseat that started to smoke as she wriggled suggestively across it.

Even during the height of burlesque, the Block still maintained a family side, just one that became more discrete. Bernard Livingston recalled growing up with a father who ran the Clover starting in the 1930s:

> *Our unofficial residence was the ticket box. On Friday, my mother would take the Sabbath dinner to the ticket box and light the Sabbath prayer candles. She hung a mezuzah on one of the posts inside. It was only about 4 or 5 feet, but sometimes the whole family was there, all seven children.*[213]

When his father died in 1944, Livingston's mother continued to operate the club before selling it in 1947. Livingston didn't go into the family business. He grew up to join the army and pass the bar, while one of his brothers became a doctor at Johns Hopkins. He claimed this illustrated that even with all of the striptease surrounding his childhood, his family was "well adjusted." It's remarkable considering the Clover, and its neighbor the Globe, were both some of the lowest varieties of burlesque, considered "scratch-houses," referring to the vermin that scratched away inside. All day, they showcased old movies and amateur strippers—or peelers—to a piano player and drummer. Miles (Cohen) Murphy and Billy (Dutch) Schultz performed as comedians at the two venues for decades. During various intermissions of all the shows, "filthy books, pictures and novelties" would be offered to the audience of "sailors, seamen, dockers, industrial works and teen-age kids."[214]

If a sailor coming to port found a girl he really liked on the Block, he may have visited one of its various tattoo parlors to have her name forever inscribed on his bicep. Charles J. Geizer, also known as "Tattoo Charlie," was a regular fixture in the area, and his studio still operates, although he passed away years ago. Proud of his art, Tattoo Charlie claimed to have given tattoos to thousands of people over the years, including inscribing an anchor on Prince Edward, the Duke of Windsor.[215] Perhaps this was during one of the times the duke came to visit Wallace Simpson, the Baltimore divorcée he abdicated the British throne to marry in 1937.

If a person didn't like going to Tattoo Charlie's, he could always go to Einar "Tattoo Bill" Kluge or Frenchy Sommers, although most just referred to Sommers by his first name. Despite having lost several fingers on his left hand, he still managed to tattoo with a rare deftness of skill. He even tattooed a dog's nose once, so that it would place in competitions. Apparently, the dog took several ribbons after the small white mark was "removed."[216]

As cities changed, televisions appeared in more homes and the sexual revolution started, the Block evolved—or perhaps devolved—into a darker version of itself. The businesses interspersed between the theaters moved to other areas, replaced by harder versions of adult entertainment, including "adult book-shops, peep shows, and show bars." Fights were not uncommon. Stephen Hull wrote about an experience he encountered at the Oasis in the mid-1950s:

> On the writer's last visit, a liquor glass, hurled by an irate female guest at Willie Gray, the m.c., grazed his (the writer's) scalp before thudding into the bosom of a vocalist known as Battleship Maggie, who was standing beside Willie. Maggie, whose chief forte is singing an obscene ballad called "Hot Nuts," didn't seem to mind. When a disturbance seems imminent at the Oasis, "Kid Shoofly" takes over. The Kid comes out of a bottle behind the bar and his real name is Michael Finn. He generally quiets things down. If he doesn't, Machine-Gun Butch [a female bouncer] comes in. Butch

plays pretty rough. Neither Kid Shoofly nor Butch had much to do during Max [Cohen]'s regime, for Max was a fast talker and generally got people to see things his way. On one occasion, he forestalled a hold-up of the club by persuading the heisters that the hold-up concession was held by the house.[217]

The women in the clubs began taking off more than the law allowed, and gambling grew more prevalent. In 1961, authorities charged Julius "Lord" Salsbury with tax evasion. Salsbury had taken over the Oasis from the Cohens and used it as a front for various racketeering operations. After spending time in prison and being shot by a former employee, he eventually sold the club and disappeared. His whereabouts are still unknown.

Although some of the personalities and entertainers continued to invest in the area, the atmosphere surrounding the Block changed. Icons like Blaze Starr tried to keep the spirit of the Block intact. She purchased the Two O' Clock—the same place she started in the city. However, viewership dwindled, and she sold the building in 1974.[218]

Nonetheless, Starr was one of the great striptease artists who came from the Block's twilight years and remains well known today. When she first showed at the Twelve O'Clock in the 1950s, "Miss Spontaneous Combustion" was only a young teenager. However, she appeared older than she was, perhaps thanks to her famous dimensions of 38D-24-37. "I hadn't yet turned 16, but I dressed so I looked really grown up," explained Starr. "I wore a short black skirt and held a long cigarette holder."[219] Originally Fannie Belle Fleming of West Virginia, Starr soon found herself a hot commodity on the traveling circuit. She became embroiled in an affair with Louisiana's governor, Earl Long, and claims to have had "a quickie in a closet with Jack [President John F. Kennedy]."[220] She "hung up her g-string" well into her fifties—long after most other strippers had retired. Her eponymously titled autobiography was turned into a movie starring Paul Newman. She finally retired to her home state of West Virginia, where today she sells jewelry online.

For the past several decades, old-timers have lamented the passing traditions of the Block. Irma the Body, who regularly played the Gayety, complained:

Stripping is a lost art. There's nothing to get curious about when you see a stage full of naked women. You gotta tease a little, with a sexy outfit. A bra, high heels, a garter belt and stockings. Then peel them off slowly. That's what starts their hearts pumping.[221]

The Block. *Historic American Buildings Survey, Library of Congress.*

They probably would have retained mixed feelings if they visited the Block today. Although the buildings are in good tradition, the shows are not the same tame fare served in earlier years. Burlesque remains a vital tradition in the city. Neo-burlesque performers like Trixie Little and the Evil Hate Monkey and Paco Fish and Gilded Lily Burlesque have strong cult followings. Little even organized a show on the Block itself at the Hustler Club, although these groups tend to perform in other venues throughout Baltimore. The night at the old Gayety Theater beautifully merged the past with the present, as newbie visitors cheered on the Hustler Honeys, and the Honeys placed tips in the g-strings of the old-school performers.[222]

Although the Gayety Show World and some of its surrounding buildings remain burned-out shells, the Block today continues to bump and grind its way forward. No matter how many officials have attempted to shut it down, how many people have complained about the loss of the "tease" or how the visitors have changed, the Block continues to thrive, like a phoenix that rises out of its ashes.

The Battle over Liquid Bread

Baltimore and Prohibition

There can be little doubt that Baltimore enjoys a good drink. After all, this is the city where a neon-lit Mr. Boh—the mascot of locally based National Bohemian beer—watches over all with his singular eye from the tower in the Brewers Hill neighborhood. Baltimore is also the home of the Horse You Came In On Saloon in Fells Point, which purports to be the oldest continuously operating bar in the country, dating back to 1775. And this is the hometown of H.L. Mencken—the man who helped lead the fight against Prohibition through so many editorials of the *Evening Sun*. Maryland, after all, is not known as the "free state" due to patriotic stances during the Revolutionary or Civil War but because it refused to pass any state laws enforcing Prohibition.

While saloons, taverns and bars were commonplace in Baltimore, locals also enjoyed the neighborhood barrelhouse. "A barrel house was a saloon to which customers came with bottles, jugs, pitchers and even pans, and bought whisky and wine direct from big kegs that lined the walls," explained George Reus Jr. in an article for the *Sun* in 1952. Reus was the son of a former barrelhouse owner and had worked there as a kid. His family's barrelhouse had a regular saloon upstairs and a cellar filled with over two hundred barrels of various types of alcohol. They kept ninety-eight on tap. According to him, whiskey ran from two to five dollars a gallon, while brandy was "sixty cents a quart, gin never more than seventy-five cents, and wines, like sherry, port, muscatel and tokay, were less than fifty cents." Barrelhouse owners kept their prices down by purchasing certificates directly from distillers. The certificate would be purchased at the same time as the whiskey was created but used a few years later, after the drink had properly aged.[223]

Even with this strong alcohol-laced history, the battle over Prohibition started early here. A conference of Methodist ministers met in 1784 at Lovely Lane Church to discuss, among other things, the issue of temperance. It was an important subject to many groups, particularly abolitionists, throughout the nineteenth century. When the arguments reached their height in the early twentieth century, Baltimore was at the forefront of the debate. In the days leading up to the vote on Prohibition in 1916, groups—including the Anti-Saloon League of Maryland and United Temperance Forces of Maryland on one side and the Association Against the Prohibition Amendment on the other—ran nearly endless campaigns of advertisements, letters to the editors, articles and editorial cartoons in Baltimore's newspapers, trying to win over the voters.

The Association Against the Prohibition Amendment included advertisements in all of Baltimore's major newspapers. These ads took a variety of tactics, appealing to different voter fears regarding health, taxes and immigration. Like the ads run by their opponents, these ads showcased a strange array of propaganda, facts and misinformation. One read:

> *Mr. Voter—Prof. Charles F. Chandler, Chemist of Columbia University, says: "Beer is one of the few foods free from bacteria. Beer and Bread are both made from cereals, and yeast makes both palatable and digestible." Food, Drink, and Health unite in beer. Ask your doctor! VOTE AGAINST PROHIBITION.[224]*

Countering these arguments was Reverend T.M. Hare, superintendent of the Anti-Saloon League of Maryland. In a letter to the editor of the Sun on Thursday, September 28, 1916, Reverend Hare endorsed being "dry" and showcased other cities as an example of the prosperousness that Baltimore might attain if it went in the same direction. He wrote:

> *Baltimore need not be afraid of prohibition. The same results will follow there that have followed in Birmingham, Denver, Portland and Seattle—all large cities. The fact is that if Baltimore will vote itself dry, it will receive much more advertising than it received when the submarine landed at that*

A Vote Against Prohibition sign in Fells Point. *Author photograph.*

port and many people will visit the city to see the largest city in the United States that by its own efforts threw off the curse of the organized liquor traffic with its demoralizing influences and its great economic waste.[225]

The parade of arguments for Prohibition did little to impress columnist H.L. Mencken; he found them all to be cold and boring. He dismissed them quickly as unlikely to sway any voters. "As a citizen of Baltimore and Maryland, and entitled to certain inalienable rights thereby, I protest publicly against the introduction of a deadly dreariness into the prohibition campaign," lamented Mencken in the *Evening Sun* on October 31, 1916. He went on to say how he had expected the same over-the-top show that the Anti-Saloon League had put on during its campaign against liquor in West Virginia. With gleeful sarcasm, Mencken felt he could finally "praise" Dr. Hare when Hare announced that a "grand prohibition dress parade and cavalcade" would arrive in Baltimore. Mencken said that he looked forward to the promised "parades, scandals, challenges, fights, arsons, raids, warrants,

H.L. Mencken, by Carl Van Vechten, 1932. *Carl Van Vechten Photograph Collection, Library of Congress.*

pinwheels, coffin-wagons, boozers in cages, sky rockets, [and] red fire." How unfortunate, it seemed to him, that the fireworks had been delayed "until the last minute."

Prohibition eventually passed in 1919, and Maryland became the sixth state to ratify the new law. However, the state refused to pass a local enforcement act. Because it was the only state not to do so, Congressman William D. Upshaw derided Maryland as traitorous. In response, Hamilton Owens, editor of the *Sun*, lambasted him in a 1923 editorial called "The Maryland Free State." Owens mocked Upshaw by suggesting that Maryland should indeed secede. He didn't print the column, but he did begin to use the nickname. It caught on and remains popular today.

Even though many bars did close during this time, several others continued to thrive, including the Owl Bar, which operates today in the Belvedere Hotel in Mount Vernon. Patrons could forgo "near-beer" and partake of the real variety if they knew the pass phrase: "The wise old owl sat on an oak, the

The Belvedere Hotel.
Author photograph.

more he saw, the less he spoke, the less he spoke, the more he heard." The owl in the bar had eyes that would blink, letting the patrons know they could safely enjoy their drinks. If the eyes stopped blinking, then the party was temporarily over.

On the eve of Prohibition's end in April 1933, Mencken was invited to the Rennert Hotel to celebrate its repeal. As the clock struck midnight, the crowd heaved around him, waiting to see his reaction to the first legal drink in thirteen years. He downed the beer handed to him in a single gulp and said, "Pretty good, not bad at all. Fill it again."

Largely because of its disinterest in enforcing Prohibition laws, the mob never took control of Baltimore like in Chicago or Atlantic City. It wasn't until well after Prohibition ended that notorious gangster Al Capone found his way to the area. When Capone was released from jail in 1939, he immediately headed to Baltimore. However, the reason he came had nothing to do with alcohol, money or anything else criminal. He came because he thought he might be dying, and he saw his one last hope in the city.

The story starts several years earlier. Before Capone became the legendary Scarface, he was a young neighborhood rough who frequented prostitutes. Perhaps this is where he contracted what his doctors called "paresis," an old euphemism for an even older disease: syphilis. Either way, he was officially diagnosed while in prison, having been convicted for tax evasion. While he had experienced earlier flare-ups from the disease, he had been unaware that even though the symptoms might die down, the infection never completely went away.

Capone came to Baltimore because of Union Memorial Hospital. While being treated there, a rumor floated around that he was living at 5708 Pimlico Road, not far away in the Mount Washington neighborhood. This was a trick, according to Captain Menasha E. Katz. In reality, the gangster was actually living with him. Katz had met Capone's lawyer in 1935 at the Bismarck Hotel in Chicago while attending a governors' convention. He was surprised when the lawyer called him in 1939, months before Capone was even released from prison. He recalled the conversation in a 1975 article for the *Sun*:

> *Early in 1939—I think Capone was still in Alcatraz—I got a long-distance call from the lawyer. He just wanted to renew our acquaintance, he said. There didn't seem to be anything else on his mind. Apparently he just wanted to see if I was still around.*[226]

In November, Capone was paroled. He had served seven and a half years of an eleven-year sentence. He immediately headed to Baltimore. The following day, Katz got another phone call. This time, it was from Harry Smart, who was the one who actually did live at 5708 Pimlico Road. Capone, under the name of Rozzi, did stay there temporarily, but someone thought it would be best if he was moved. "I don't know if they'd planned it that way from the beginning, or if they began to fear for his life and changed plans accordingly," reported Katz. He agreed to let Capone and both of his bodyguards take the second floor of his house, which was also on Pimlico. However, the tomfoolery with the press continued:

> *It was reported in The* Sun *that somebody representing Al Capone went to a real estate agent and tried to rent an apartment in Guilford* [another

124

neighborhood] *for him and his family at $250 a month. When the agent saw who the client was, so the story went, he backed out. Then the representative offered another real estate man $300 a month put Capone up in a Guilford apartment and got turned down.*[227]

Katz confirmed that none of it was true; Capone wanted to be left alone and was staying with Katz at the time. He described his house as private, with a "10-foot hedge around it, and there was a barn, garage, and other outbuildings. It was the perfect place for an out-of-towner to live unnoticed." He explained that he often rented out rooms, especially to the "jockeys and trainers when the horses were running at Pimlico [Race Track]." As such, no one would notice out-of-state license plates. Even his family was in the dark about the true identity of their houseguests.[228]

When Capone arrived, he came in style, riding in a "1931 or 1932 bulletproof Lincoln." He wasn't the larger-than-life character that most people saw. He had slimmed down to 165 pounds and was obviously sick. He kept to himself, and Katz didn't engage with him regularly, although he did share one story:

I said to him: "My little girl thinks you look like Edward G. Robinson." He grinned a little and said: "Don't tie me in with that guy." I saw him face to face only another time or two, and that was about as much as he ever said in front of me.[229]

Capone soon checked into Union Memorial Hospital under the name "Mr. Martini." He was treated for several months before being released in March 1940. He moved to Florida and died in 1947. In a gesture of gratitude, he donated two large cherry blossom trees to the institution. Since donating the trees, one was removed for hospital construction, and the other was damaged during a major snowstorm in February 2010. It still flourishes today. Many Baltimoreans enjoyed their beautiful blossoms for decades—most without even knowing their true history.

Nor was Capone the only icon of the Roaring Twenties who sought medical assistance in Baltimore as Prohibition dwindled down. In 1932, Zelda Fitzgerald, the quintessential flapper and wife of F. Scott Fitzgerald—himself the second cousin three times removed of Francis Scott Key—sought respite multiple times in the city. Her husband wrote *Tender is the Night* in the charming,

Tree given by Al Capone to Union Memorial Hospital. *Author photograph.*

brick-lined neighborhood of Bolton Hill while she sought treatment at Johns Hopkins University and then sojourned in Sheppard Pratt, a mental health facility that still operates near Towson. She finished her own autobiographically inspired novel, *Save Me the Waltz*, while here. In a letter to F. Scott when he was away, Fitzgerald wrote, "I love Baltimore. The shops are very sophisticated, and there is amusement without end if you were here and we could amuse ourselves without bothering about cures."[230] She would remain in and out of mental treatment facilities until her death in 1948 in a fire at Highland Hospital in North Carolina.

Baltimore is almost unique when it comes to Prohibition. While there were certainly plenty of "drys" in town, overall the city didn't want the restriction and was one of the wettest places in the nation. Unlike other previous volatile issues, Baltimore didn't react by rioting or using any of the other violent techniques it had employed in the past. Instead, the city just decided to ignore the restriction and continued to do what it believed to be right: drinking its heart out.

Notes

PREFACE

1. Russell Baker, "The Biggest Baltimore Loser of All Time," *New York Times*, October 21, 1973.

BANISHING WILLIAM GODDARD

2. Proclamation by the House of Delegates, April 18, 1777, MS 1814, Maryland Historical Society (MDHS).
3. Frederick N. Rasmussen, "An 18th-Century Dynamo," *Sun*, June 26, 1999.
4. Scharf, *History of Maryland*, 306.
5. Legion "Notes" to William Goddard, March 3–4, 1777, MS 1814, MDHS.
6. Ibid.
7. Proclamation by the House of Delegates.
8. W. Bird Terwilliger, "William Goddard's Victory for the Freedom of the Press," *Maryland Historical Magazine* 36, no. 2 (1941): 143.
9. Ibid., 139–49.
10. Scharf, *History of Baltimore*, 780.
11. Lee, *Life and Memoirs*, 154–55, 157.
12. Wroth, *History of Printing*, 139.
13. Scharf, *History of Baltimore*, 780.
14. Wroth, *History of Printing*, 139.

NAPOLEON'S SISTER-IN-LAW

15. MDHS, MS 142.
16. Burns, *Betsy Bonaparte*.
17. Didier, *Life and Letters*, 7.
18. "Madame Patterson-Bonaparte," *McBride's Magazine* 20 (1877): 310.
19. Burns, *Betsy Bonaparte*, 42–43.
20. Browning, *American Historical Register*, 583.
21. MDHS, MS 142.
22. Ibid.

AMERICA'S OLDEST OPERATING PENITENTIARY

23. There is debate about whether a penitentiary in Russia may be older. See Shugg, *Monument to Good Intentions*, ix–xii. While the Eastern State Penitentiary is no longer operating, it still stands and has been turned into a museum.
24. Olson and Brown, *Some Gave All*, 3–4; Scharf, *History of Maryland*, 201.
25. Shugg, *Monument to Good Intentions*, 125.
26. *Sun*, March 6, 1953; February 25, 1955
27. Ibid.
28. Ibid.
29. Ibid.
30. Alexander Gifford, "Murder in Prison's Shadow," *Baltimore News Post*, April 16, 1936; *Sun*, May 5, 1890.
31. *Sun*, May 5, 1890.
32. *Sun*, December 30, 1890; June 12, 1891.
33. Maryland Division of Correction Annual Report, 27.

THE BIRTH OF MOBTOWN

34. Beirne, *Amiable Baltimoreans*, 145.
35. Scharf, *History of Baltimore*, 782.
36. Ibid.; Beirne, *Amiable Baltimoreans*, 145–46.
37. *Hampden Federalist*, August 13, 1812.

38. "Narrative of Mr. John Thomson."
39. Ibid.
40. Ibid.
41. Ibid.
42. Ibid.

Nest of Pirates

43. Eshelman, Sheads and Hickey, *War of 1812*, 55.
44. Barney, *Biographical Memoir*, 11–13.
45. George, *Terror on the Chesapeake*, 11–12.
46. Barney, *Biographical Memoir*, 255.
47. Ibid., 256.
48. Ibid.
49. Beirne, *Amiable Baltimoreans*, 177.

A Terrible Trade

50. Power, *Impressions of America*, 35.
51. Steffen, *Mechanics of Baltimore*, 6.
52. Douglass, *Narrative*, 39–40.
53. Ibid., 329.
54. Ibid., 55.
55. *New York Daily Tribune*, July 30, 1863.
56. Watkins, *Narrative*, 9–10.
57. Stanton Tierman, "Baltimore's Old Slave Markets," *Sun*, September 13, 1936.
58. Clayton, *Cash for Blood*, 59.
59. Ibid., 61.
60. *Niles' Weekly Register* 32 (1827).
61. Ibid.
62. Douglass, *Life and Times*.

WOULD POE HAVE BEEN POE WITHOUT BALTIMORE?

63. Quinn, *Edgar Allan Poe*; Thomas and Jackson, *Poe Log.*

64. Ibid.

65. Ibid.

66. Ibid.

67. Ibid.

68. *Saturday Visiter* 2, no. 27 (August 4, 1832): 3, Maryland Historical Society, www.eapoesociety.org.

69. Quinn, *Edgar Allan Poe*; Thomas and Jackson, *Poe Log.*

70. Hewitt, *Recollections of Poe*, 19.

71 Quinn, *Edgar Allan Poe*; Thomas and Jackson, *Poe Log.*

72. Moran, *Defense of Edgar Allan Poe.*

73. Edgar Allan Poe Society, "The Mysterious Death of Edgar Allan Poe," http://www.eapoe.org/geninfo/poedeath.htm (accessed on May 18, 2011).

74. Moran, *Defense of Edgar Allan Poe*, 59.

75. Benitez, "Rabies," 765–69; http://www.umm.edu/news/releases/news-releases-17.htm (accessed May 18, 2011).

76. Edgar Allan Poe Society, "Testing Poe's Hair," http://www.eapoe.org/geninfo/poethair.htm (accessed May 18, 2011).

77. Moran, *Defense of Edgar Allan Poe*, 55.

78. "Ludwig" (Rufus Wilmot Griswold), "Death of Edgar A. Poe," *New-York Daily Tribune*, October 9, 1849, http://www.eapoe.org/papers/misc1827/nyt49100.htm (accessed on May 18, 2011).

79. Walsh, *Midnight Dreary.*

80. Sartain, *Reminiscences of a Very Old Man*, 206–07.

81. Ibid.

82. Walsh, *Midnight Dreary.*

83. Powell, *Too Much Moran.*

84. Scarlett, "Tale of Ratiocintation."

85. Scharpf, "Where Lies a Noble Spirit?" 194–222.

86. Edward Petit, "We're Taking Poe Back," *Philadelphia CityPaper*, October 2, 2007, http://archives.citypaper.net/articles/2007/10/04/were-taking-poe-back (accessed on May 18, 2011).

87. "Philadelphia, Baltimore Battle Over Edgar Allan Poe," National Public Radio, October 31, 2007, http://m.npr.org/news/front/15817021?page=1.

Plug Uglies, Blood Tubs and Rip Raps, Oh My!

88. *Sun*, August 9, 1839.

89. Ibid.; Scharf, *History of Baltimore*, 786.

90. Ibid.

91. Melton, *Hanging Henry Gambrill*; *Sun*, June 25, 2003.

92. *Sun*, October 17, 1857.

93. *Washington Star*, June 4, 1857.

94. Melton, *Hanging Henry Gambrill*, 43, Lewis Allen, *City in Slang*, 211.

95. *The Plug Uglies!!*, American Song Sheets, Rare Book and Special Collections Division, Library of Congress, 1857.

96 Beirne, *Amiable Baltimoreans*, 337.

97. Ibid.

98. Scharf, *History of Baltimore*, 786

99. Both Americans went on to continue violent careers. In 1857, Boney Lee, a Rip Rap, assaulted *Sun* reporter Hanna over an article he had written in the paper. Lee tried attacking Hanna with his billy stick, but Hanna ducked and went for his pistol. Before he could shoot, Lee disappeared. Hanna was arrested, at which point Lee resurfaced and punched him, with the police officer still present. Lee was also arrested, but both were released.

100. Melton, *Hanging Henry Gambrill*, 91–93; *Sun*, October 9, 1856.

101. *Sun*, October 9, 1856.

102. Ibid., November 6, 1856.

103. Ibid., September 9, 1859.

104. Ibid., "When Baltimore Was Known as 'Mobtown,'" April 20, 1958.

105. Ibid., September 21, 1859.

106. *Evening Sun*, "City Police Power to Issue Scrip Born of Election Riots 80 Years Ago," December 6, 1939.

107. Melton, *Hanging Henry Gambrill*, 307–08.

108. *Frank Leslie's Illustrated Newspaper*, "A Maryland Outrage—A Philadelphia Train Attacked in Baltimore on the Eve of the Pennsylvania Election," October 12, 1868.

109. Ibid.

The Baltimore Plot

110. *Sun*, November 7, 1860.

111. Pinkerton, *Spy of the Rebellion*, 59.

112. Ibid., 63.

113. Ibid., 68.

114. Ibid., 68–69.

115. Ibid., 71.

116. Kline, *Baltimore Plot*, 170.

117. *Alleged Hostile Organization Against the Government within the District of Columbia*, February 1861, 2, 132–134.

118. Pinkerton, *Spy of the Rebellion*, 85.

119. Brown, *Baltimore and the Nineteenth of April*, 11.

120. Ibid., 11–12.

121. Lamon and Black, *Life of Abraham Lincoln*, 512–13.

122. Ibid., 517.

123. Brown, *Baltimore and the Nineteenth of April*, 44–45.

124. *Sun*, April 20, 1861.

125. Brown, *Baltimore and the Nineteenth of April*, 49.

126. *Sun*, April 20, 1861.

127. Ibid.

128. Ibid.

129. Ibid.

130. http://www.msa.md.gov/msa/mdmanual/01glance/html/symbols/lyricsco.html (accessed May 28, 2011).

"Revolt on the Railroads"

131. Announcement from B&O Railroad, July 11, 1873, B&O Railroad Museum.

132. Fee and Shopes, *Baltimore Book*, 3.

133. *Sun*, July 17, 1877.

134. Scharf, *History of Maryland*, 732.

135. *Sun*, July 21, 1877; Scharf, *History of Maryland*, 734.

136. *Baltimore American and Commercial Advertiser*, July 23, 1877.

137. *Sun*, July 21, 1877; Scharf, *History of Maryland*, 734.

138. *Sun*, July 21, 1877.

139. Ibid.

140. Scharf, *History of Maryland*, 739.

141. *Baltimore American and Commercial Advertiser*, July 23, 1877.

142. *Journal of the Proceedings of the House of Delegates of Maryland* (January 1878): 1406.

143. Governor John Lee Carroll, *Message of John Lee Carroll, Governor of Maryland, to the General Assembly*, January 1878, 20.

144. Fee and Shopes, *Baltimore Book*, 11–12

Did She or Didn't She?

145. *Sun*, July 12, 14 and 17, 1871.

146. Ibid.

147. Ibid.

148. Ibid., July 13, 1871.

149. Ibid.

150. Ibid.

151. Ibid., July 12, 1871.

152. Ibid., July 17, 1871.

153. Ibid., August 14, 1871.

154. Ibid., July 17, 1871.

155. Ibid., July 25, 1871.

156. Ibid., July 17, 1871.

157. Ibid.

158. Ibid., December 4, 1871.

159. Ibid., May 19, 1890.

160. Ibid., January 8, 1872.

161. Ibid., January 26, 1872.

162. Ibid., July 11, 1879.

163. Ibid., May 19, 1890.

Burking, Bodies and Baltimore

164. *Sun*, December 14, 1886.

165. *West Port Murders*, 217–18.

166. *Sun*, December 13, 1886.
167. Ibid., August 4, 1907.
168. Ibid., December 13, 1886.
169. Ibid.
170. Ibid., February 5, 1887.
171. Ibid., August 4, 1907.
172. Ibid., January 22, 1887.
173. Ibid., June 22, 1887.
174. Ibid., August 4, 1907.
175. Ibid.

Playing "Winder"

176. *Sun*, December 23, 1906.
177. Ibid., March 21, 1906.
178. Ibid., March 31, 1906.
179. Ibid., March 21, 1906.
180. Ibid., March 30, 1906.
181. Washington, *Story of the Negro*, 364.

The Sordid Findings of Baltimore's Vice Commission

182. Baltimore Vice Commission Report, Vol. 1, 1915, 75.
183. Ibid., 105.
184. Ibid., 109.
185. Ibid., 76.
186. Ibid., 193.
187. Ibid., 76.
188. Ibid., 77.
189. Ibid., 70.
190. Ibid., 77.
191. Ibid., 140.
192. Ibid., 71.
193. Ibid., 176.

194. Mencken, *Book of Prefaces*, 246.

195. *Sun*, December 22, 1915.

196. Woolston, *Prostitution in the United States*, 234.

197. Report of the Board of Police Commissioners for the City of Baltimore, 1915, 13.

198. O'Meally, *Lady Day*.

199. Fagan, Dufty and Pelote, *Lady Sings the Blues*.

200. http://archive.mdhs.org/eubieblake/subs/06.html (accessed May 16, 2011).

The Block

201. Bob Litwin and Chip Silverman, "An Affectionate History of Burlesque," *Baltimore Magazine* (August 1979).

202. *Sun*, December 15, 2010.

203. Ibid., February 9, 1907.

204. http://www.mdch.org/fire (accessed May 28, 2011).

205. Litwin and Silverman, "Affectionate History of Burlesque."

206. Eckhardt, *King of the Movies*, 61–62.

207. *Sun*, January 24, 1971.

208. Ibid.

209. Hull, "Baltimore's Bawdy Block."

210. *Sun*, May 31, 1970.

211. Litwin and Silverman, "Affectionate History of Burlesque."

212. Ossman, *Built to Last*.

213. Earl Arnett, "Burlesque House Box Office Once Served as Home," *Sun*, April 16, 1971.

214. Hull, "Baltimore's Bawdy Block."

215. *Sun*, May 21, 1978.

216. Edward Maxwell, "They Let the War Get Under Their Skins," *Sun*, September 1, 1940.

217. Hull, "Baltimore's Bawdy Block."

218. Ossman, *Built to Last*.

219. Sellinger, "Stripper Blaze Starr."

220. Ibid.

221. Litwin and Silverman, "Affectionate History of Burlesque."

222. Greg Hanscom, "Bump and Grind: What Happens When Burlesque Comes Back to Baltimore's Red-Light District?" *Urbanite Magazine*, July 1, 2009.

THE BATTLE OVER LIQUID BREAD

223. George G. Reus Jr., "That Varnished Institution Called the Barrel House," *Sun*, August 17, 1952.

224. *Sun*, September 7, 1916, MDHS.

225. MDHS

226. Katz, "I Remember."

227. Ibid.

228. Ibid.

229. Ibid.

230. Bryer and Barks, *Dear Scott, Dearest Zelda*, 151.

Bibliography

Primary Sources, Archives

B&O Railroad Museum files
Edgar Allan Poe Society files
Enoch Pratt Free Library vertical files
Library of Congress files
Maryland Historical Society MS files
National Public Radio

Autobiographies

Brown, George William. *Baltimore and the Nineteenth of April 1861: A Study of the War*. Baltimore, MD: N. Murray, 1887.

Douglass, Frederick. *Autobiographies: Narrative of the Life of Frederick Douglass, an American Slave; My Bondage and My Freedom; Life and Times of Frederick Douglass*. New York: Literary Classics of the United States, 1994.

Fagan, Eleanora, William Dufty and Vincent Pelote. *Lady Sings the Blues*. New York: Doubleday, 1956.

Pinkerton, Allan. *The Spy of the Rebellion: Being a True History of the Spy System of the United States Army during the Late Rebellion Revealing Many Secrets of the War Hitherto Not Made Public*. New York: G.W. Carleton, 1886.

Starr, Blaze, and Huey Perry. *Blaze Starr: My Life*. N.p.: Praeger, 1974.

Watkins, James. *Narrative of the Life of James Watkins*. N.p.: Kessinger Publishing, 1853. Reprint, 2004.

NEWSPAPERS

Baltimore American and Commercial Advertiser

Baltimore News Post

Baltimore Sun

Frank Leslie's Illustrated Newspaper

Hampden Federalist

New York Daily Tribune

New York Times

Niles' Weekly Register

Philadelphia CityPaper

Saturday Visiter

Washington Star

REPORTS

Baltimore Vice Commission Report. Vol. 1. 1915.

Maryland Division of Correction Annual Report. Fiscal Year 2010.

"Narrative of Mr. John Thomson, One of the Persons Intended to be Massacred with General Lingan and Others, in the Gaol of Baltimore, on Tuesday, the 28th of July Last." 1812.

Report of the Board of Police Commissioners for the City of Baltimore. 1915.

SECONDARY SOURCES

Barney, Mary. *A Biographical Memoir of the Late Commodore Joshua Barney: From Autographical Notes and Journals in Possession of His Family, and Other Authentic Sources*. Boston: Gray and Bowen, 1832.

Beirne, Francis F. *The Amiable Baltimoreans*. New York: E.P. Dutton & Co., 1951.

Benitez, Dr. R. Michael. "Rabies." *Maryland Medical Journal* 45 (September 1996).

Browning, Charles, ed. *The American Historical Register*. Vol. 3. Boston: Historical Register Publication Company, 1896.

Bryer, Jackson R., and Cathy W. Barks, eds. *Dear Scott, Dearest Zelda: The Love Letters of F. Scott and Zelda Fitzgerald*. New York: St. Martin's Griffin Edition, 2003.

Burns, Helen Jean. *Betsy Bonaparte*. Baltimore: Maryland Historical Society, 2010.

Chalkley, Tom, Charles Cohen and Brennen Jensen. *Charmed Life*. Baltimore: Woodholme House Publishers, 2000.

Clark, Dennis Rankin. "Baltimore, 1729–1829: The Genesis of a Community." PhD diss., Catholic University of America, 1976.

Clayton, Richard. *Cash for Blood: The Baltimore to New Orleans Domestic Slave Trade*. New York: Heritage Books, 2002.

Didier, Eugene Lemoine. *The Life and Letters of Madame Bonaparte*. New York: C. Scribner's Sons, 1879.

Eckhardt, Joseph P. *The King of the Movies: Film Pioneer Siegmund Lubin*. N.p.: Fairleigh Dickinson University Press, 1997.

Elfenbein, Jessica I., John R. Breihan and Thomas L. Hollowak. *From Mobtown to Charm City: New Perspectives on Baltimore's Past*. Baltimore: Maryland Historical Society, 2002.

Eshelman, Ralph E., Scott S. Sheads and Donald Hickey. *The War of 1812 in the Chesapeake: A Reference Guide to Historic Sites in Maryland, Virginia, and the District of Columbia*. Baltimore, MD: Johns Hopkins University Press, 2010.

Fee, Elizabeth, and Linda Shopes. *The Baltimore Book: New Views of Local History*. Philadelphia: Temple University, 1991.

Forrest, Clarence H. *Official History of the Fire Department of the City of Baltimore: Together with Biographies and Portraits of Eminent Citizens of Baltimore*. Baltimore, MD: Williams & Wilkins, 1898.

George, Christopher. *Terror on the Chesapeake: The War of 1812 on the Bay*. Shippensburg, PA: White Mane Books, 2000.

Griswold, Rufus Wilmot (aka "Ludwig"). "Death of Edgar A. Poe." *New-York Daily Tribune*, October 9, 1849.

Hanscom, Greg. "Bump and Grind: What Happens When Burlesque Comes Back to Baltimore's Red-Light District?" *Urbanite Magazine*, July 1, 2009.

Hewitt, John Hill. *Recollections of Poe*. Atlanta, GA: Emory University, 1949.

Hill, Jayme Rae. "From the Brothel to the Block: Politics and Prostitution in Baltimore During the Progressive Era." Master's thesis, University of Maryland, Baltimore County, 2008.

Hull, Stephen. "Baltimore's Bawdy Block." In *America's Cities of Sin*. N.p.: Stag, 1952.

Katz, Menasha E. "I Remember…Al Capone Hiding." *Sun*, December 7, 1975.

Keire, Mara L. *For Business & Pleasure: Red-Light Districts and the Regulation of Vice in the United States, 1890–1933*. Baltimore, MD: Johns Hopkins University Press, 2010.

Kline, Michael J. *The Baltimore Plot: The First Conspiracy to Assassinate Abraham Lincoln*. Yardley, PA: Westholme Publishing, 2008.

Lamon, Ward Hill, and Chauncey Black. *The Life of Abraham Lincoln: From his Birth to his Inauguration as President*. Vol. 2. Boston: J.R. Osgood and Company, 1872.

Lee, General Charles. *Life and Memoirs of the Late Major General Lee, Second in Command to General Washington*. New York: Richard Scott, 1813.

Lewis Allen, Irving. *The City in Slang: New York Life and Popular Speech*. N.p., n.d.

Litwin, Bob, and Chip Silverman. "An Affectionate History of Burlesque." *Baltimore Magazine*, August 1979.

Maryland Historical Magazine

Melton, Tracy Matthew. *Hanging Henry Gambrill: The Violent Career of Baltimore's Plug Uglies 1854–1860*. Baltimore: Maryland Historical Society, 2004.

Mencken, H.L. *Book of Prefaces*. New York: Alfred A. Knopf, 1917.

Milford, Nancy. *Zelda: A Biography*. New York: Harper Perennial Modern Classics, 2011.

Mitchell, Charles W. *Maryland Voices of the Civil War*. Baltimore, MD: Johns Hopkins University Press, 2007.

Moran, John J. *A Defense of Edgar Allan Poe: Life, Character and Dying Declarations of the Poet. An Official Account of His Death*. N.p.: W.F. Boogher, 1885.

Okrent, Daniel. *Last Call: The Rise and Fall of Prohibition*. New York: Scribner, 2010.

Olson, Steven P., and Robert P. Brown. *Some Gave All: A History of Baltimore Police Officers Killed in the Line of Duty, 1808–2007*. Baltimore, MD: Fraternal Order of Police Memorial Fund Committee, 2007.

O'Meally, Robert G. *Lady Day: The Many Faces of Billie Holiday*. New York: Da Capo Press, 1991.

Ossman, Laurie, PhD. *Built to Last: Gayety Theatre*. Washington, D.C.: Historic American Buildings Survey, 2002.

Osteen, Mark, and Frank J. Graziano. *Music at the Crossroads: Lives & Legacies of Baltimore Jazz*. Baltimore, MD: Apprentice House, 2010.

Powell, Michael. *Too Much Moran: Respecting the Death of Edgar Poe*. N.p.: Pacific Rim University Press, 2009.

Power, Tyrone. *Impressions of America: During the Years 1833, 1834, and 1835*. Vol. 2. Philadelphia: Cabet, Lea, & Blanchard, 1836.

Quinn, Arthur Hobson. *Edgar Allan Poe, A Critical Biography*. New York: D. Appleton-Century Company, 1941.

Rockman, Seth. *Scraping By: Wage Labor, Slavery, and Survival in Early Baltimore*. Baltimore, MD: Johns Hopkins University Press, 2009.

Rodgers, Marion Elizabeth. *Mencken: The American Iconoclast*. Oxford, UK: Oxford University Press, 2007.

Sartain, John. *The Reminiscences of a Very Old Man, 1808–1897*. New York: D. Appleton & Company, 1899.

Scarlett, Charles, Jr. "A Tale of Ratiocintation: The Death and Burial of Edgar Allan Poe." *Maryland Historical Magazine* (1978).

Scharf, John Thomas. *History of Baltimore City and County, From the Earliest Period to the Present Day: Including Biographical Sketches of their Representative Men*. Philadelphia: L.H. Everts, J.P. Lippincott & Co., 1881.

———. *History of Maryland: From the Earliest Period to the Present Day*. Vol. 1. Baltimore, MD: J.B. Piet, 1879.

Scharpf, Christopher. "Where Lies a Noble Spirit? An Investigation into the Curious Mystery of Edgar Allan Poe's Grave in Baltimore." In *Masques, Mysteries, and Mastodons: A Poe Miscellany*. Baltimore, MD: The Edgar Allan Poe Society, 2006.

Sellinger, Margie Bonnett. "Stripper Blaze Starr Recalls Her Affair with the Governor." *People* 32, no. 25 (December 18, 1989).

Shalhope, Robert E. *The Baltimore Bank Riot: Political Upheaval in Antebellum Maryland*. Urbana: University of Illinois Press, 2009.

Shivers, Frank R. *Maryland Wits & Baltimore Bards: A Literary History with Notes on Washington Writers*. Baltimore, MD: Johns Hopkins University Press, 1998.

Shugg, Wallace. *A Monument to Good Intentions: The Story of the Maryland Penitentiary, 1804–1995*. Baltimore: Maryland Historical Society, 2000.

Steffen, Charles. *The Mechanics of Baltimore: Workers and Politics in the Age of Revolution, 1763–1812*. Urbana: University of Illinois Press, 1984.

Stockett, Letitia. *Baltimore: A Not Too Serious History*. Baltimore, MD: Johns Hopkins University Press, 1997.

Thomas, Dwight, and David K. Jackson. *The Poe Log: A Documentary Life of Edgar Allan Poe, 1809–1849*. Boston: G.K. Hall & Co., 1987.

Walsh, John Evangelist. *Midnight Dreary: The Mysterious Death of Edgar Allan Poe*. New Brunswick, NJ: Rutgers University Press, 1998.

Washington, Booker T. *The Story of the Negro: The Rise of the Race from Slavery*. Vol. 2. New York: The Outlook Company, 1909.

West Port Murders: or, An Authentic Account of the Atrocious Murders Committed by Burke and his Associates. London: Oxford University, 1829.

Woolston, Howard B., PhD. *Prostitution in the United States*. New York: The Century Company, 1921.

Wroth, Lawrence. *A History of Printing in Colonial Maryland*. Baltimore, MD: Typothetae of Baltimore, 1922.

About the Author

Lauren R. Silberman is a program coordinator with the American Association of Museums and served as the education coordinator for the Jewish Museum of Maryland in Baltimore. She has also given local tours with Baltimore Tours, LLC. A graduate of George Washington University, she previously authored *The Jewish Community of Baltimore* (Arcadia Publishing, 2008). She lives with her husband and dog. In her free time, she loves to paint and write. You can learn more about her and her projects at www. lsilberman.com.

Lauren Silberman, by Will Kirk.
Author collection.